The Power and Problem of Forgiveness

Trevor Chandler

Sovereign World

Sovereign World Ltd
PO Box 777
Tonbridge
Kent TN11 9XT
England

First published 1980
Sovereign World Edition 1994
Copyright © 1994 Trevor M. Chandler

ISBN: 1 85240 147 8

Typeset by CRB (Drayton) Typesetting Services, Norwich.
Printed in England by Clays Ltd, St Ives plc.

Acknowledgements

This is the second edition of this book. When it was originally completed it was my first attempt at serious writing and the task would not have been done without the encouragement and help of members of my own congregation at Christian Life Centre, Brisbane, Australia.

In the first edition my thanks were expressed to those who had assisted me in checking and correcting the original draft and for suggestions to improve expression. My deep appreciation to them remains, and I would mention Kath Filmer-Davies, Keith Smith, Cheryll Greer, Shirley Lloyd, Peter Clyburn, Chris Attwood and Bob Blair.

My wife Sylvia had been willing to spend days and evenings alone to allow the work to be completed, and I will always be grateful for her support and encouragement.

The purchase of a lap-top computer gave me the incentive during overseas travel to tackle the task of revising the material with a view to reprinting. The original quantity published had been comparatively small, and the first edition has been out of print for some years, but I have regularly received requests for the book.

Lurline Bennett, a missionary teacher and college professor stationed in Shizuoka Province, Japan, has undertaken the task of editing this second edition and I am deeply grateful for her professional assistance and practical comments in presenting this material for republication.

All scripture references have been changed to The New International Version unless otherwise stated.

Dedication

This book is dedicated to all those who long to be free from the burden of unforgiveness, and although they have wrestled with the problem, have been unable to find a practical answer to genuinely forgiving from the heart.

Trevor Chandler

Contents

Dictator or Directed?
A Mind Made Up!
Signs and Symptons

Introduction

I have always been amazed and thrilled by the grace of God, His mercy, forgiveness and pardon. I have not fully understood how God would be so beneficent in spite of man's sin and constant failure, but I have accepted His wonderful provisions with a grateful heart.

Some people find it hard to accept that God could so freely forgive sin and failure, and so they remain with a sense of guilt and condemnation. Or, if they do accept that God has forgiven them, they find it hard to forgive themselves. Because of this, people live without the joy and peace that they should have.

Others live a life of self pleasing and indulgence with the idea that they need only ask God to forgive them and He will immediately do so, and the consequences of any violation or sin will be cancelled.

It has been my conviction for several years that many of our beliefs and concepts about forgiveness have been inadequate and faulty, and that people have treated the matter of forgiveness either too lightly or considered that the implications of forgiveness were beyond their capacity to meet.

My experience has shown that the majority of people can accept God's forgiveness of them, but they lack the knowledge and understanding to genuinely forgive others who have wronged or hurt them. They know that Jesus said that if we do not forgive others God will not forgive us, but this knowledge, rather than solving the problem, increases their burden of guilt.

This book is an endeavour to throw light upon the problems that many people have with understanding and implementing forgiveness. When we do understand how to forgive we will be in a position to receive the positive benefits which come as a result of forgiving others as God has forgiven us.

Trevor Chandler

'Seek the Lord while he may be found; call on him while he is near.

Let the wicked forsake his way and the evil man his thoughts. Let him turn to the Lord, and he will have mercy on him, and to our God, for he will freely pardon.

"For my thoughts are not your thoughts, neither are your ways my ways," declares the Lord.

"As the heavens are higher than the earth, so are my ways higher than your ways and my thoughts than your thoughts.

As the rain and snow come down from heaven and do not return to it without watering the earth and making it bud and flourish, so that it yields seed for the sower and bread for the eater,

so is my word that goes out from my mouth: It will not return to me empty, but will accomplish what I desire and achieve the purpose for which I sent it."'

(Isaiah 55:6–11)

Chapter 1

The Foundation of Forgiveness

We had talked for about twenty minutes. Her story was one of heartbreak and despair: a young wife and mother suddenly deserted by her husband. There was a look of hopelessness on her face! She said, 'Are you telling me that I must forgive a man who walked out on our child and me to be with another woman? How can I do that? Do you know what it means to watch the last cent every week and cry yourself to sleep because of loneliness?'

Why This Subject?

This experience and many others which have come from counselling people over the years, have made me aware of the deep problems in the lives of so many men and women which demand the exercise of forgiveness. There have been hurts and wounds so deep, that it seems almost impossible for them to forgive; but I am also aware that there is, through the ability to forgive, a tremendous benefit for good in a person's life. A lack of forgiveness, however, will bring much that is harmful spiritually, mentally and physically. People have lost their reality of God, are emotionally and mentally in turmoil and physically sick, because of bitterness that comes as a result of unforgiveness.

There is, through the ability to forgive, a tremendous benefit for good in a person's life.

Our lives are interwoven with those of others and we are involved in interpersonal relationships every day, and as a result, many situations which give rise to misunderstanding or offence occur. It is essential that we understand fully what is involved in the subject of forgiveness.

This book has been titled *The Power and Problem of Forgiveness* because there is great power for good in our lives if we can genuinely forgive, but there is a great problem in being able to do it! It would be easy to give a list of scriptures based on what the Bible says about forgiveness, but that would not guarantee an answer to our problem. We can know what is right but not know how to do it. I want to unfold this subject step-by-step to the point that we know exactly what forgiveness is, and also how to forgive.

There is a great power for good in our lives if we can genuinely forgive, but there is a problem in being able to do it!

Let me refer to two brief passages of scripture. The first is in the Old Testament:

'Seek the Lord while he may be found; call on him while he is near.

> *Let the wicked forsake his way and the evil man his*
> *thoughts.*
> *Let him turn to the Lord, and he will have mercy on*
> *him, and to our God, for he will freely pardon.'*
>
> (Isaiah 55:6–7)

The second says:

> ' *"This, then, is how you should pray:*
> *'Our Father in heaven, hallowed be your name, your*
> *kingdom come, your will be done on earth as it is in*
> *heaven.*
> *Give us today our daily bread.*
> *Forgive us our debts, as we also have forgiven our*
> *debtors.*
> *And lead us not into temptation, but deliver us from*
> *the evil one.'*
> *For if you forgive men when they sin against you, your*
> *heavenly Father will also forgive you. But if you do*
> *not forgive men their sins, your Father will not for-*
> *give your sins."'*
>
> (Matthew 6:9–15)

The latter part of this scripture, which deals with the effect that our forgiving others has upon God's forgiveness of us, is particularly challenging and is an important aspect of our studies. We will, however, deal with this in detail in a later chapter.

Three Vital Words

We need to lay a foundation by examining three words that are essential to our understanding of this topic. The words are:

Mercy   Forgiveness   Pardon

Jesus said quite clearly that we were to forgive one another. He did not qualify the particular cause. He did not say, 'If it is a small hurt, then forgive.' He did not say, 'If it is a large hurt, it is different.' He made a plain statement and told us to forgive one another.

Quoting scripture is not difficult, neither is giving lip service to a truth. But when we have been hurt and wounded by the action of another, we can know that we should forgive, and yet feel totally unable to do it.

We all find that the actions of other people create some of the greatest difficulties with which we have to contend. No man lives unto himself. What others say and do has a bearing upon our lives almost every day. In the course of our relationships with people, many things happen to us: actions and words that are unkind, inconsiderate and hurtful. We may experience lies told about us, betrayal by friends and other injustices. Reactions may occur and ill-will develops within us.

When we have been hurt and wounded by the action of another, we can know that we should forgive, and yet feel totally unable to do it.

Let me ask a question, not as a preacher or Bible teacher but as a man who knows what it is to go through this kind of experience. 'How can a person genuinely and honestly forgive when confronted by problems of this kind?' It is easy to say we should forgive, but it is not so easy to do it!

I was conducting a series of special meetings in New Zealand, and one night was speaking about the problem of inferiority and a negative self-image. At the end of the sermon I gave opportunity for any suffering from such problems to come forward for prayer. A number of people responded, and the first person to whom I went was a teen-age Maori girl. I did not ask any details about her problem, but as I placed my hand on her head, I found myself praying in an unusual way. I said, 'You are a daughter of God! You are a child of the King!'

I repeated these statements several times, much to my own amazement, and the tears began to trickle down the girl's face. It was obvious that the Holy Spirit was doing a work within her. I moved on, praying for others, and soon the meeting closed.

Prior to the service the next night, the young woman concerned approached me with an amazing testimony which she later shared in part with the whole congregation. This is what she said:

When I was several years younger, my older sister had been extremely jealous and hateful. On one occasion my sister said, 'I cannot bear you to touch me! Don't ever put your hand on me. Even if I am dead, do not touch me, or I will sit up and spit in your face!'

As a result of this experience I had a sense of worthlessness and a deep inner hurt. Later I committed my life to Christ and was baptized with the Holy Spirit, but the feelings of insignificance and inferiority remained. Last night for the first time in my life, I was able to recognize that I was important to God, and I really was his daughter. I have been set free, and at last have been able to forgive my sister.

If we know what the Bible says, then two things are likely to happen. The first is that we can become make-believers because we cannot do what the Bible says but pretend to do it. Jesus said, 'Forgive one another.' We are hurt! We are wounded! Because we are hurt it seems impossible to forgive, but because the Bible says we should, we pretend that we have obeyed this command, but bitterness remains within and we have become make-believers. The second thing that can happen is that we come under condemnation, because we are trying to be honest and know we should forgive, yet find ourselves failing to do it and so have a sense of guilt as a result.

The subject of genuine forgiveness has many sincere Christians in confusion. In the letter to the Hebrew Church we read:

> *'See to it that no one misses the grace of God and that no bitter root grows up to cause trouble and defile many.'* (Hebrews 12:15)

Many people are suffering because of bitterness which has entered their lives through unforgiveness. Forgiveness can lift burdens and restore friendships. It can bring peace and joy to a person's life whereas unforgiveness can cause bitterness, hatred, discord, turmoil and sickness. The greatest percentage of the problems that we go through are our own fault! We are reaping what we have sown.

The subject of genuine forgiveness has many sincere Christians in confusion.

The principle of sowing and reaping is related to forgiveness, and although we are enjoying fellowship with

God, we may still be reaping from the seeds of sin and disobedience we have sown. One of the truths we will cover in some detail later is that it is possible to be forgiven, to enjoy fellowship with God, and yet still be under the discipline of God! We need to understand the subject of forgiveness in all its aspects, so that we may know how to genuinely obey the Word of God, and find a place of freedom as we live our daily lives.

Forgiveness is not a simple subject! It has not been fully understood by many people and only a genuine knowledge of what it is, how it operates, and how God sees it, will enable us to appropriate the benefits of true forgiveness. Time must be taken to lay sound foundations to bring us to a clear understanding of the subject and to allow the principles to be absorbed and established in our lives.

The essential starting point is to understand the meaning of the three words which have been mentioned: mercy, forgiveness, and pardon. These words are often thought of synonymously, and of course they can be related, but they are essentially different. In considering these terms in a spiritual sense I want to define each one.

The essential starting point is to understand the meaning of the three words which have been mentioned; mercy, forgiveness and pardon.

What Do They Mean?

Mercy is the exercise of less severity than one deserves, or it is the granting of kindness and favour beyond what one may rightly claim.

Forgiveness dismisses resentment or displeasure from the heart of the one offended, and in particular it has reference to feelings and fellowship.

Pardon completely remits the outward penalty which the offender deserves. It is the act of a superior toward an inferior implying the right to punish. It deals with the consequences of an action. Pardon is an executive responsibility which most people do not have the right to exercise.

These three attributes of mercy, forgiveness, and pardon are included in the character of God. The Bible says He is a God who shows mercy, who forgives, and who will abundantly pardon.

Let me confirm this from scripture:

> *'The Lord, the compassionate* (merciful) *and gracious God, slow to anger, abounding in love and faithfulness.'*
> (Exodus 34:6)

> *'Let him turn to the Lord, and he will have mercy on him, and to our God for he will freely pardon.'*
> (Isaiah 55:7)

Mercy, forgiveness, and pardon are all part of the nature and attributes of God, but we must also understand that God's character includes righteousness, truth, and justice.

There are conditions and responses which God requires when we are dealing with these matters of mercy, forgiveness, and pardon. Perhaps it is correct to say that there is nothing that we receive from God that is unconditional apart from His grace.

God showers His grace upon people, but from that point on, all the dealings of God towards us are in response to actions or attitudes taken or made by us. Mercy and forgiveness on their own, without the inclusion of pardon, do not automatically remove all the consequences of sin and failure.

I know that some people reason like this: 'If God has been merciful to me, the problem is over.' That is not correct! They think, 'If God has forgiven me, then the record is wiped clean.' That is not correct! There would have to be the inclusion of pardon before a complete result was achieved so we can have a genuine operation of mercy and forgiveness and yet not have the removal of the consequences of certain sins.

Mercy and forgiveness on their own, without the inclusion of pardon, do not automatically remove all the consequences of sin and failure.

All of these attributes of God's mercy, forgiveness and pardon must be taken into consideration, not just some of them. Our actions are going to bring forth certain results, so we need to know how God in His total character will respond to what we have done, and even to our request for forgiveness.

Why Should I Let Him Off?

Perhaps we have been unwilling to be merciful and forgiving because we think that a serious repeated offender will be let off, and so we will allow some injustice to continue. If someone has repeatedly offended us, we might think to ourselves, 'If I do not take some positive action against him, but am merciful and forgiving, then he will go on doing this. I cannot forgive him because this would mean excusing his action.'

We must realize that this is a wrong attitude, because we do not have the right to take over the executive responsibilities that go with pardon. Mercy and forgiveness do not automatically include pardon so it is not our responsibility to take punitive action against an offender. That is God's responsibility! A person can receive mercy and forgiveness by God but still suffer effects in his life because he has not met the requirements for full pardon. One of the vital requirements to receive forgiveness and pardon from God is that we forgive those who have wrongfully treated us. If we don't forgive, we can continue to suffer in our own relationship with God.

Because an understanding of these principles is at the heart of this book let me make clear that showing mercy and granting forgiveness are our responsibilities when problems arise with other people, but pardoning is God's responsibility.

A young man gave me this testimony:

> At the age of nine years I sat in the back of a bus waving goodbye to my mother and brother. I loved my brother deeply, but there was a deep hatred within me towards my mother who had arranged for me to live with foster parents. I decided as I sat in that bus that I would never forgive her, no matter what happened!
>
> As I grew older my hatred grew! I did not have what the other boys around me had. I hated my foster parents because they had been party to my being separated from my brother. I became a rebel in society. I was taken to different psychiatrists and they would talk to me about my attitude toward my

mother. I had no power to change my hatred and those interviews seemed to increase my bitter feelings.

When I was sixteen years of age my brother came to visit me. From him I obtained my mother's address and wrote several letters asking her to visit me. I had a deep motive of hatred in writing to her. When she came I said, 'I hate you and will never forgive you!'

Nine years later I accepted Jesus Christ as my Saviour and was baptized in water and with the Holy Spirit. It was a revolutionary experience, but my Christian life fluctuated and there were days of joy and victory, but also days of defeat and despair. Something was wrong.

One night I listened to a visiting preacher speaking on the subject of forgiveness. He said, 'We must put away all hatred, we must forgive our mother if necessary.' I knew that the Holy Spirit was speaking to me! I felt that the Lord was saying, 'I will not open your life completely to me until you learn to forgive.'

I determined to put things right and travelled over a thousand miles to the city where my mother lived to tell her that I forgave her and loved her. I was released from what seemed like chains binding me, and found a new purpose and consistency in my Christian life.

Today, the man who gave this testimony is an elder in one of the churches belonging to the group of churches with which I am associated. It has been a blessing for me to see the continued growth in his life, his cheerful

Christian zeal, and to see the way that he and his wife have established a fine family.

One of the vital requirements to receive forgiveness and pardon from God is that we forgive those who have wrongfully treated us.

What I am saying in this chapter may be a new concept to some Christians, but we must face the reality of these issues and extend mercy and forgiveness to others and leave the pardoning to God, otherwise the dealings of God can continue in a judgmental way upon our lives although God has been merciful and has forgiven us.

If we do not understand what happens when God forgives us, then we will be confused. People have said to me, 'I know my heart is right with God. I have asked Him to forgive me, but I do not understand why these problems are continuing in my life.'

Problems can arise for various reasons. One of the reasons is because we are still reaping what we have sown, and another is because God is allowing us to go through His dealings for the development of our lives. There are other reasons as well, so we must learn to determine whether we are violating some principle of God or whether He is disciplining us for our own good and development. In a later chapter we will discover how we can know the difference between being under the judgmental hand of God although we have been forgiven, and going through the dealings of God to refine our character for His purpose.

> *The dealings of God can continue in a judgmental way upon our lives, although God has been merciful and has forgiven us.*

Understanding Mercy

I want to deal now with the subject of mercy, because that is where the foundation of forgiveness begins. We need to realize first of all that God's mercy is subject to certain limitations. There is a general mercy of God that applies to all mankind. The Bible says:

> *'He causes His sun to rise on the evil and the good, and sends rain on the righteous and the unrighteous.'*
> (Matthew 5:45)

Have you ever wondered why a godly man and an ungodly man both have their crops growing and prospering in the same way? God declares that He gives a general mercy to all His creation. The sun shines on the righteous and also on the unrighteous. The rain falls on the good and also on the evil. Everybody in this world is in some measure under the merciful dealings of God. The psalmist says:

> *'The Lord is good to all; he has compassion on all he has made.'*
> (Psalm 145:9)

The Bible does not say that He has compassion or mercy on some of His creation but on **all** of it. Irrespective of our situation, we are all receiving more than we justly deserve. God, however, has special blessings for those who are obedient to what He says and He

27

prospers those who give according to His word. In the Book of Malachi God says that if we bring our tithes into the storehouse He will open the windows of heaven and pour out such a blessing that there will not be room enough to receive it.

There are special blessings, but there are also general blessings, and all people, even though they may be atheistic or blaspheme the Name of God come under the merciful provisions of a loving God. I want to call this 'temporal mercy'. Temporal means 'to be confined to this natural life or this earth', so there is the mercy of God that applies to us while we are living in this world. God bestows this mercy so that a person may respond to Him. A person can look around and see the beauty of the world, the provisions that have been made, and in so doing recognize that the mercy of God is extended towards him, but this mercy does not extend beyond the person's earthly life. We have a responsibility to recognize God from his creation and His graciousness to us. The apostle Paul in writing to the church in Rome said:

> *'For since the creation of the world God's invisible qualities – his eternal power and divine nature – have been clearly seen, being understood from what has been made, so that men are without excuse.'*
>
> (Romans 1:20)

We read often of the miraculous ways that God has intervened to save committed Christians from death or injury. I have heard testimonies and read the stories of men and women wonderfully protected in air crashes, road accidents, or shipwrecks, experiences that obviously were due to divine protection.

God declares that He gives a general mercy to all His creation.

Hebrews chapter 11 tells of the men and women of faith who were miraculously helped by God, but it also tells of others who suffered torture, imprisonment, and death. Yet the scripture says that all of these, those who experienced miracles of deliverance and those who did not, were commended for their faith! God is merciful, but He has a plan that He is working out for our lives and we cannot guarantee the degree of mercy or deliverance that will be provided in any situation of life. What God does unconditionally promise, however, is the grace to cope with whatever circumstance may arise.

I was in business as an Insurance Loss Adjuster and Assessor at the time of a disastrous flood which occurred in the city and surrounding areas of Brisbane, in 1974. It would be wonderful to report that no Christians suffered in that cyclone and flood, but that would not be a true account. In that disaster some buildings were completely submerged, homes and business premises were destroyed, millions of dollars of damage was done, and lives were lost. Homes and businesses belonging to both Christians and non-Christians were affected. I saw Christians weep as they reported how their precious possessions were carried out of their homes a sodden mess, but I did not doubt God's ability to supernaturally sustain them in their sorrow and loss and later to make other provisions to re-establish them in life.

We cannot, however, guarantee that protection and good will always be the lot of the Christian, while the non-Christian suffers. We need to understand that in addition to the temporal mercy of God there is also an eternal mercy. Eternal mercy is subject to right responses on our part to God. The Psalms record this statement:

> *'But from everlasting to everlasting the Lord's love is with those who fear him, and his righteousness with their children's children – with those who keep his covenant and remember to obey his precepts.'*
>
> (Psalm 103:17–18)

There is a temporal mercy of God available to all, but there is an everlasting mercy as well. This everlasting mercy is for *'those who fear him ... who keep his covenant and remember to obey his precepts.'* A person may enjoy the mercy of God in this natural life, but we can also make sure that we enjoy the mercy of God *'from everlasting to everlasting!'*

We cannot, however, guarantee that protection and good will always be the lot of the Christian, while the non-Christian suffers!

Remember very carefully that mercy is not the same as forgiveness. Mercy is the exercise of less severity than a person deserves, or it is the granting of a kindness beyond what one may claim. Men and women are commanded to be merciful and to be forgiving. They are not commanded to pardon. In a spiritual sense, and in most of the events of life, we do not have the right or privilege to pardon. It is God, not men and women, who deals with consequences!

In the different societies and nations in which we live there are laws. To some people there may be given the responsibility of exercising those laws with some degree of discretion. By way of an example, if we break the law and a policeman sees us, he has no right to excuse our offence. His reponsibility is to enforce the law of the land. If, because of that offence we are later taken to court, the magistrate or judge may be able to exercise an authority that the policeman did not have, and he might say, 'I have considered all the circumstances, and in this instance I intend to pardon you.' Or it may be that the right of pardon rests only with a person such as a governor, president, king or queen. There are certain executive positions that carry with them the power and right to pardon, but we as ordinary people have been commanded by God to be merciful and forgiving, irrespective of what may happen in regard to pardon.

I want to emphasize that being merciful does not mean being soft or easy going. It does not mean pretending that something has not happened. I know that such an attitude would suit a world that wants to destroy absolutes and be ruled by situation ethics. It is easy to say, 'I'm not hurting others so I can please myself.' People say, 'Moral values are different now. We don't have to accept the standards of our parents.' Someone else says, 'It's a good cause so the end justifies the means!'

The concept of situation ethics can be summed up by the words of what became a popular song, 'It can't be wrong when it feels so right.' The issue of de facto relationships is a case in point. The Bible teaching in both Old and New Testaments very clearly shows that such relationships are sinful. Those involved in these relationships, however, will always be ready to justify them. 'I needed a roof over my head,' 'This was my only chance for happiness,' 'We love each other,' 'A piece of paper does not make our love any more real.'

The same reasoning can be seen in the arguments for abortion. 'Let a woman have the power to decide what to do about her own body,' the feminists and those who demand freedom of choice cry as they wave their banners. The Bible tells us plainly that our bodies are not our own, but God's, and the foetus is not the woman's own. On the grounds of nervous tension, financial stress, or simply 'I don't want to have another baby,' abortion is chosen and the seriousness of the destruction of the unborn child is justified by these reasons. The other alternatives such as adoption or even better, trusting God, are not seriously considered. I do not seek to minimize the problems that arise from unwanted pregnancies but we must learn that we cannot violate the Word of God without consequences being involved.

Situation ethics are applied in everyday life by people who take advantage of a telephone breakdown to make free long distance calls, who keep extra change given by mistake in some shop, who take pencils, erasers, rulers and stationery from their places of employment. 'It's all right,' they say, 'the telephone company/the government/the boss can afford it, and I can't.' All of these are examples of flagrant disregard for God's law justified, albeit poorly, by the need of a person at that time.

Recently I found amongst my papers a set of duplicated notes on the subject 'A Basis for Morality.' The author is unknown so I am unable to give an acknowledgment, but part of the article is relevant to what is presented here so I quote:

> Even though all have not succumbed to the Permissive Society, we must all confess that we are

surrounded by it and sometimes, perhaps, we are influenced by its pragmatism. Pragmatism means broadly 'if what I do makes me happy then it is right.' In other words, morality is made subjective to experience.

To bolster the pragmatic approach, in the words of one psychologist, it is necessary to 'damn the absolutes.' And where and what are the absolutes? They are the final statements of society on moral behaviour chiefly written into the laws of the land.

These laws of western society find their roots in the Ten Commandments. Hence the final attack on the absolutes must be on the Bible itself. This attack looked like being successful up to midway into this century. However, since that time a remarkable event has taken place. God sent the Charismatic Renewal which, as well as being a subjective spiritual experience, has for its basis the objective truths and absolutes of the Word of God.

Modern society may well yet turn to the Church for guidance in moral matters when it finds that its idol of permissiveness is an idol with clay feet.

God is merciful, but mercy does not mean a docile agreement with what men and women want to do. Mercy is not being soft. Far from it!

Mercy and Truth

When studying the scriptures relating to mercy, I found that the word most associated with mercy was truth. Mercy and truth! We cannot have genuine mercy without the operation of truth! The scripture makes this declaration:

'By mercy and truth iniquity is purged.'

(Proverbs 16:6 KJV)

Iniquity is not purged by mercy alone; it is purged by the operation of both mercy and truth together. We are mistaken if we think of mercy at the expense of truth or law.

True mercy, however, involves a sense of pity and concern, and an action to relieve the suffering. If we merely look with sympathy at some situation, then that is not mercy. Mercy must do something in a practical and tangible way to meet the need. There have been occasions when I have felt sympathetic about a situation but I have done nothing about it. I have not shown mercy; I have been sympathetic.

I have looked at pictures of starving children and read appeals for help. I have read stories of disaster and famine and felt a desperation at the plight of the people. I have read about hardship, persecution, and imprisonment of Christians in Communist-dominated countries. There was a genuine sense of sympathy, but only when I took some action, either in giving or praying, was there an operation of mercy.

We are mistaken if we think of mercy at the expense of truth or law.

A clear illustration of mercy is found in the parable which Jesus told of the Good Samaritan. A Jewish traveller was attacked by thieves and robbers and was left lying on the side of the road bleeding and bruised. Two people, one a priest and the other a Levite, went by and passed on. They looked at the wounded and needy man but took no action. Then the Samaritan came. The Samaritan did not have any obligation to the wounded Jew. He was of a different race of people. Samaritans were despised by the Jews, but this Samaritan went to the aid of the injured traveller and began to bind up his wounds. He helped the man and took him to an inn and paid the bill for the injured man's accommodation. The Samaritan said to the inn-keeper, 'Look after him and if it costs any more I will pay it when I return' (Luke 10:35).

The injured man had no legal claim on the Samaritan. This Jew had no rights that he could demand, but the Samaritan out of mercy towards him reached out and gave him something that he could not legally claim. That is an example of genuine mercy: going beyond what a person has a legal right to expect. Let me give another illustration, this time from my own experience.

The girl was neither attractive nor particularly likeable. She had been rebellious in her home and gone her own way. Her mother was a dedicated Christian but in spite of a good family example, the daughter turned to drugs, alcohol, and tobacco and finally was admitted to a mental hospital for treatment. On her discharge from hospital, she became an infrequent attender at the church where I was the pastor, but there was little about the girl to evoke sympathy as her selfish attitude was still very evident.

Her sister was to be the bridesmaid at a wedding and an invitation to attend the reception was given to the family. The girl, because of lack of work, had little money, and the mother lived on a 'bread line' budget. The wedding invitation posed a problem as the girl did not have suitable clothing to wear. One of the women in the church took the girl into the city and purchased for her a complete outfit of clothing. It was a spontaneous act of love and generosity when no duty or responsibility rested upon the giver.

Mercy and Judgment

Mercy does not, however, eradicate all judgment. Another key parable of Jesus that relates to this topic is found in Matthew's Gospel. This story is known as The Parable of the Unjust or Unmerciful Servant. The parable tells of a servant who owed his master a large amount of money. He was called before the master to give an account of his debt. The Bible record gives this account:

> '*Since he was not able to pay, the master ordered that he and his wife and his children and all that he had be sold to repay the debt.*
> *The servant fell on his knees before him. "Be patient with me," he begged, "and I will pay back everything."*'
> (Matthew 18:25–26)

Will you note that the servant did not ask for forgiveness of the debt; he did not ask for pardon from the debt; he asked for mercy! What he asked for was an extension of time to meet the amount that was owing. The master would have been merciful had he done just that. He would have been going beyond what was his legal right to demand.

Mercy does not, however, eradicate all judgment.

36

In this particular parable, however, the master did not stop with an expression of mercy but he went on to forgive the man, and also to pardon him of the total debt. We read:

> *'The servant's master took pity on him, cancelled the debt and let him go.'*   (Matthew 18:27)

This parable shows the operation of mercy, forgiveness, and pardon, although the servant asked only for mercy.

The servant who had received this undeserved provision then went out and laid hold of a fellow servant who owed him a small debt, and demanded immediate payment. The Bible tells that the second servant asked for mercy and said, 'Give me time to pay' (Matthew 18:29). The first servant denied the request for mercy, the very thing that had been given to him, and he had the second servant thrown into prison. When the master was told of what had happened he called the first servant and rebuked him and said:

> *'I cancelled all that debt of yours because you begged me to. Shouldn't you have had mercy on your fellow servant just as I had on you?'*   (Matthew 18:32–33)

The master then revoked the pardon, forgiveness, and mercy that he had previously extended to the first servant. Let me emphasize, that if we are going to understand how to forgive we must first learn to be merciful, because forgiveness is a step beyond mercy. If we do not learn to be merciful, we will never be forgiving! Mercy comes first, then forgiveness follows.

We must recognize that if we will not extend mercy to

others, the mercy that has been extended to us may be rescinded. Every believer in the Lord Jesus Christ is required to be merciful. It is the foundation stone of forgiveness. If we do not learn to be merciful then it is certain that we will never be able to forgive from the heart. We may appear to have some success in forgiving a person with whom we have had a dispute and think that we have won the battle to forgive, but some conflict with that person will again arise, and the old hurt will be felt once more.

If we are going to understand how to forgive, we must first learn to be merciful.

We must begin where God begins, and that is at the place of mercy. None of us has a right to demand his 'pound of flesh'. Every one of us is obliged by God's Word to extend some degree of mercy according to the situation that might apply.

No Retribution

Jesus, in his teaching, completely did away with the right of equal retribution. It is not a matter of saying, 'You did that to me, I will do the same to you.' Jesus said:

> *'You have heard that it was said, "Eye for eye, and tooth for tooth." But I tell you, do not resist an evil person. If someone strikes you on the right cheek, turn to him the other also.*
> *And if someone wants to sue you and take your tunic, let him have your cloak as well.*
> *If someone forces you to go one mile, go with him two miles.'* (Matthew 5:38–41)

The Christian does not have the right to demand exact retribution at the level of what he has received. If we are to exercise mercy, then we cannot demand an exact legal penalty, but we must reach out with some understanding and kindness.

A paraphrase of James 3:1 could be expressed as, be careful about becoming teachers or leaders. The more you know of the will and ways of God, the greater will be your responsibility. If you are a Christian and have known the Lord for, say, one week, and commit a particular sin, and if some more mature Christian should commit the same sin, the standard of God's mercy will be different. The new Christian will receive a higher level of mercy than the experienced Christian, because the mature person has the benefit of greater knowledge by which he could judge his own actions.

The Word of God makes clear that the more we know the greater is our accountability, because mercy is not measured by the same yardstick. It is measured by the circumstances, our background, and our understanding.

Let me give a simple illustration of how we might apply mercy in a practical way. If you lent someone $100 on the condition that he would repay by a particular date, and when that time came, he was not in a position to pay, what then would be a merciful thing to do? To genuinely extend mercy, all that you would need to do would be to say, 'I will give you another week to pay.' If you gave even one extra day you would have been merciful. It would have been to a small degree, but there would have been mercy, because the debt was legally due prior to that time. Every day given beyond the due date would be an extension of mercy.

To be merciful does not demand that one forgoes or

reduces the debt. By the mere provision of additional time one has met the requirements of mercy. If, however, you said, 'Instead of $100, pay me $90,' you would then have gone beyond mercy to forgiveness and a measure of pardon. If you said, 'God has blessed me so I want to cancel the debt,' you would have been merciful, forgiving, and pardoning.

Mercy is not measured by the same 'yardstick'. It is measured by the circumstances, our background, and understanding.

Let us clearly understand the difference in these terms. It is so important that we recognize these aspects because God's mercy does not necessarily remove His judgments.

The dealings of God can continue in our lives even when God has been merciful, but, because of His character, He always reduces the severity of what we should rightfully receive, so the mercy of God is the beginning of forgiveness. It may also be the beginning of pardon, but the provisions of mercy, forgiveness, and pardon are separate steps, and each one may require a different response from us in order to receive them.

God does not require any response from us before He is merciful. Whenever we call on the Lord we can expect Him to be merciful, but before He forgives, and pardons, there may be some responses that we have to make. We can always approach God and He will deal with us with less severity than we deserve, and that is a marvellous truth to know! Mercy, however, is always linked with truth and righteousness. God will not violate His Word but will show compassion, and we will always get more consideration from Him than that to which we should be entitled.

God has been merciful to us, so let us in turn be merciful to others. Don't try to give the same treatment that you have received. If we give tit for tat, we have failed at the first step which is to be merciful. Don't demand equal satisfaction. That might make a person feel justified but it will ultimately destroy him.

The provisions of mercy, forgiveness, and pardon, are separate steps, and each one may require a different response from us in order to receive them.

We have no right to equal retribution if we are going to be merciful, because it is not our duty to punish. It is God who judges, punishes, and pardons. Being merciful is a first step to sincerely forgiving from the heart.

After burying his father, Joseph returned to Egypt, together with his brothers and all the others who had gone with him to bury his father.

When Joseph's brothers saw that their father was dead, they said, 'What if Joseph holds a grudge against us and pays us back for all the wrongs we did to him?'

So they sent word to Joseph, saying, 'Your father left these instructions before he died: "This is what you are to say to Joseph: I ask you to forgive your brothers the sins and wrongs they committed in treating you so badly." Now please forgive the sins of the servants of the God of your father.' When their message came to him, Joseph wept.

His brothers then came and threw themselves down before him. 'We are your slaves,' they said.

But Joseph said to them, 'Don't be afraid. Am I in the place of God? You intended to harm me, But God intended it for good to accomplish what is now being done, the saving of many lives.

So then, don't be afraid. I will provide for you and your children.' And he reassured them and spoke kindly to them. (Genesis 50:14–21)

Chapter 2

What Happened in The Old Testament?

Let us now examine the subject of forgiveness in the Old Testament, because we need to follow the whole pattern of the Word of God in order to fully understand this subject.

Was It Cruel?

There are people who consider that the Old Testament reveals a God who is harsh and cruel, but much of this thinking is due to misunderstanding. The scribes and Pharisees in the time of Jesus taught 'You shall love your neighbour and hate your enemy,' but we could search the pages of the Old Testament and not find such a statement because the Old Testament does not say it! God has always shown justice and righteousness. The scribes and Pharisees often put interpretations on the Word of God to suit themselves. The definite judgments that are set out in the Book of Exodus, particularly in chapter 21, place a limit on revenge that was so common at that time. The laws of God were not only to punish

43

for a deliberate offence but also to limit revenge. They were to establish mercy and true justice.

In primitive times an assault on one member of a particular tribe could cause a feud to break out and many people would die as a result. The law of God laid down that only the person who committed the offence could be punished, and his punishment was to be no more than the equivalent of the offence committed. There was a clear command in this regard:

> *'But if there is serious injury, you are to take life for life, eye for eye, tooth for tooth, hand for hand, foot for foot, burn for burn, wound for wound.'*
> (Exodus 21:23–25)

This was not a demand that such retribution should be exacted, but it was a limit on the demands that could be made by the offended party. A private individual was not allowed to seek personal revenge, but the law did provide a basis for an appointed judge to assess the penalty and the appropriate punishment for the offence. In other words the punishment had to be equal to the crime committed and had to be imposed by an impartial person or persons.

The laws of God were not only to punish for deliberate offence but also to limit revenge.

Who said 'Hate your Enemy?'

God never said, 'Hate your enemy!' This statement is not part of God's command. Jesus said:

> *'You have heard that it was said, "Love your neigh-*
> *bour and hate your enemy." But I tell you: Love your*
> *enemies and pray for those who persecute you, that*
> *you may be sons of your Father in heaven...'*
>
> (Matthew 5:43–44)

Jesus was not altering the law by this statement, but correcting an error that had resulted from the teachings of the scribes and Pharisees. When the scribes and Pharisees used the expression 'The Law' they could be referring to one of four things:

1. The Ten Commandments.
2. The first five books of the Bible, the Pentateuch, which to the Jews was the most important part of scripture.
3. The law and the Prophets. This expression included the whole of the Old Testament.
4. The Oral or Scribal law.

It was the oral 'law' that Jesus so often attacked! This was the supposed law of God made up from the interpretations of the scribes and Pharisees, and was not part of God's direct command. For these religious leaders everything had to be defined. Take, for example, the command *'Remember the sabbath day by keeping it holy'* (Exodus 20:8). The scribes and Pharisees had made up more than 1,500 regulations to define this command! This is why Jesus said:

> *'"And why do you break the command of God for the*
> *sake of your tradition?...*
> *Thus you nullify the word of God for the sake of your*
> *tradition. You hypocrites! Isaiah was right when he*
> *prophesied about you, 'These people honour me with*
> *their lips, but their hearts are far from me. They*

> *worship me in vain; their teachings are rules taught by men.'"'*
>
> (Matthew 15:3, 6–9)

It is also important to realize, as we study the subject of forgiveness, that God never made provision for a private individual to demand his own retribution. God did provide for wrong-doers to be punished, for God is just, but the judgment was never to be made or the penalty inflicted by the one who had been wronged. This is a very important principle to remember when we have been hurt by the actions or words of another person. Every one of us has been hurt at some time, but the principle of God is that none of us has the right to sit in judgment or inflict the punishment on the one who has offended us.

God never made provision for a private individual to demand his own retribution.

The various punishments provided by the law were not always performed literally, but the injury was assessed at its monetary value. It was based on the pain and suffering, loss of time, the indignity that had been suffered, and these factors are still the basis of the law of damages and compensation in modern times. If a person is injured today, then the law does not allow for the same injury to be inflicted on the assailant, but imposes a penalty equivalent in value to the injury, and the amount is paid to the one who has been hurt. The Old Testament is a book of mercy. We read:

> *'Do not hate your brother in your heart. Rebuke your neighbour frankly so you will not share in his guilt.*

> *Do not seek revenge or bear a grudge against one of*
> *your people, but love your neighbour as yourself. I am*
> *the Lord.'*   (Leviticus 19:17–18)

In the Book of Proverbs a statement is made that also
contradicts what the scribes and Pharisees said:

> *'If your enemy is hungry, give him food to eat; if he is*
> *thirsty, give him water to drink.'*   (Proverbs 25:21)

So often the religious leaders did not say what the Law
of God said. They gave their own interpretations.
Because God said, 'Love your neighbour' (Leviticus
19:18), they inferred that the opposite was to apply, and
so an enemy was to be hated. God does say that He
hates some particular things and also the actions of
some people, but He does not say that we are to hate
our enemies. It is so easy to jump to conclusions and
then find that our ideas are not in line with what the
Bible actually says. In the Book of Proverbs we find a
record of seven things that God says He hates:

> *'There are six things that the Lord hates, seven that*
> *are detestable to him; haughty eyes, a lying tongue,*
> *hands that shed innocent blood, a heart that devises*
> *wicked schemes, feet that are quick to rush into evil, a*
> *false witness who pours out lies and a man who stirs*
> *up dissension among brothers.'*   (Proverbs 6:16–19)

Nowhere does God say that we are to hate people!

Mercy and Justice

Examination of the various scriptures in the Old Testament that deal with forgiveness, not only reveal a God

who is merciful, compassionate, and forgiving, but also a God of justice and righteousness. True mercy is based on justice! We must learn to balance these different attributes. Where there has been an infringement making a penalty necessary, God does not pretend the offence did not happen for He is a God of truth and righteousness. When a wrong has been done then a just penalty must be imposed.

We do not have enough detail in the Bible to show us why God commanded certain severe punishments to be carried out. For example, when the people of Israel went into the land of Canaan, God commanded that they were to utterly destroy all the inhabitants of the land. I understand, from the reading that I have done, that the evil in the land of Canaan was great. There were human sacrifices and every kind of immoral act which was a complete affront to all of God's standards. The Bible declares that *'Will not the Judge of all the earth do right?'* (Genesis 18:25), and we can be sure of this, that we can trust Him. Even when our natural mind cannot understand why a particular penalty was imposed, we know that we are dealing with a just God.

The Old Testament reveals a God who is merciful, compassionate, and forgiving, but who is also a God of justice and righteousness.

God-to-Man Forgiveness

Most of the Old Testament scriptures that deal with forgiveness are either calls by individuals to God to forgive their trespasses and sins, or to thank God for forgiving them. We find, as we examine the scriptures, that it is generally a man-to-God or a God-to-man relationship which is involved. God's forgiveness is not, however, unconditional!

When people called upon God for forgiveness, although He was willing to forgive, He laid down clear conditions. These conditions were always consistent and involved repentance, confession, supplication, and often included making offerings or sacrifices as an atonement for the sin. This was a type of what was done later by the Lord Jesus Christ, when He shed His blood on the cross as an atonement for the sin of all mankind. Jesus was the Lamb of God who shed His blood as an offering for sin. However, under the Old Covenant, God provided a way in which sin could be dealt with until His final plan for salvation and forgiveness was fulfilled. So when people in Old Testament times brought an animal as a sacrifice for their sin, it was an expression of repentance and contriteness of heart. The disposition of God is always merciful and forgiving. Forgiveness was readily provided when the right conditions were met by men and women in the Old Testament.

I want to emphasize again that forgiveness and pardon are not the same. Forgiveness restores fellowship and right relationship with God, without necessarily removing the temporal consequences of a particular sin. We may be forgiven by God, restored to fellowship with Him, and yet for some time may continue to suffer the effects of the sin for which we have been forgiven. This is because of the principle of sowing and reaping that we will deal with in detail later.

To explain this, it is important for us to note that with God there are two kinds of judgment. There is temporal judgment, which pertains to the affairs of this life. It is a judgment that applies to us while we are alive on this earth. There is also eternal judgment which will have an effect upon us not only in time, but also throughout eternity.

Forgiveness restores fellowship and right relationship with God, without necessarily removing the temporal consequences of a sin.

Continuing Consequences

I have said that it is possible to continue to suffer the consequences of an action committed during our lifetime although we have been forgiven by God. This kind of judgment would not apply in eternity. It is a temporal judgment, a dealing by God in this life only. We must also remember that although a judgment may not continue on into eternity, the scriptures plainly show that by our failure to obey God, or to make right responses in different circumstances, we suffer loss, and because of this, fail to attain to the fulness of God's purpose for our lives. This does not mean that we lose our salvation, but we may have lost an opportunity to go on to God's highest purpose for our lives.

How often when faced with a crisis situation have we blamed God? We have thought that God didn't care or had forsaken us. We have asked the question, 'Why did this happen to me?' God is concerned as to how we respond even when the most difficult things happen to us.

Several years ago my wife and I had driven from

Brisbane to Sydney, a distance of over 600 miles, to conduct a series of meetings over a weekend. I was still involved in business as well as leading the church and it was important for for me to be back in my office on the Monday. We enjoyed a wonderful weekend of meetings with God's blessing being evident, and late on the Sunday evening set off to drive home through the night hours.

I was physically tired, but exhilarated by the joyous meetings. The hours moved on as we travelled homewards. By about 4 a.m. my eyes were beginning to droop! I was losing concentration. My wife had diligently stayed awake talking to me to help me keep alert while our daughter and two friends dozed in the back seat.

We should have stopped and rested. It was important to me that I was back in my office without too much delay, so my wife, who seemed wide awake, gallantly offered to take over the driving. We stopped the car and changed places.

I chatted to her for a while, but I was tired after the busy weekend. My wife was driving well; I thought that she could be travelling a little faster, but I felt safe and slipped into a partial sleep.

The sudden crash seemed unreal! I opened my eyes. The car was stopped and the bonnet was standing up in front of the windscreen.

My wife was in tears. I was suddenly awake and quickly out of the car. The front of the car was smashed in; the bonnet catch had been dislodged, and two large road marker posts were under the vehicle. We were on a bend in the road, and were now stranded on the grassy shoulder at the side. No one was injured. We looked at the scene. I felt angry! We had prayed together before leaving Sydney for a safe journey, and now this! I was not angry with my wife. She was so upset, but I was annoyed that we should be involved in an accident and now would possibly be stranded for hours.

God is concerned as to how we respond even when the most difficult things happen to us.

I had been preaching the principles of God's Word and had been encouraging people in the Bible truths of praise and worship, but at that moment I did not feel like praising God for all things.

It was much later that I realized our miraculous preservation. My wife had begun to realize that her eyes were dropping closed, but was persevering for my sake. Unconsciously she was driving more slowly, but must have lost momentary awareness as she encountered the bend in the road and the car had continued straight ahead, first striking one marker post then another. How easy it would have been to have veered into the path of vehicles coming in the opposite direction!

Two large indentations were in the front of the car where each marker post had struck. Because of the angle of the bend, one post had struck to the left of the radiator crushing the bumper bar, grill, and bonnet. The other post had struck to the right of the radiator, doing almost identical damage. We looked in amazement at the radiator and engine unaffected by the impact! Not far ahead on the same side of the road was a steep bank, and had the car left the road there, we would undoubtedly have rolled over, with possible serious results.

We managed to pull the marker posts from under the car and drove off with considerable damage to the front body, but the engine never missed a beat as we continued on our way home. I was still annoyed. I was not then thankful for an amazing escape but was still upset at the problem.

I missed an opportunity to make the right kind of response which would have allowed God to do a work of development in my character. Perhaps later problems that I have encountered were necessary because I did not allow that experience to build my trust and confidence in God at that time.

Job, in the time of his crisis was urged by his wife to curse God and die (Job 2:9). Through every kind of loss, pain, and discouragement, he maintained his confidence in God and ultimately received blessings far greater than he had previously.

The scripture makes clear that Christ is our foundation and we are to build on Him. In 1 Corinthians 3:11–15 the apostle Paul speaking symbolically says that we may build with materials of hay, wood, and stubble, but when the fire of God comes on them, they will be destroyed; but the scripture goes on to say: *'he himself will be saved, but only as one escaping through the flames'* (1 Corinthians 3:15). Salvation was still a reality for the one concerned, but he had lost what had been built on the foundation. If, to the contrary, he had built on the foundation gold, silver, and precious stones, when the fire of God came these materials would not have been destroyed, and the man would have had a lasting structure of eternal value.

Although judgment may not go on into eternity, there is a continuing loss we can suffer, if we do not build our lives on God's pattern, or make responses consistent with His Word.

Man-to-Man Forgiveness

It is important to realize that references to forgiveness in the Old Testament include only three which deal with man-to-man forgiveness. All the others are either God-to-man or man-to-God. The Old Testament is a record of people, under the law, who were entitled to the protection that the law gave them. In addition, they could demand the penalty the law provided if an offence was committed against them or their property. If a person suffered at the hands of another, he had a perfect right to say, 'Because of what I have suffered, I demand that just punishment be given to the offender.' That demand was just and right, but because the offended man could demand the penalty of the law, he was also obliged to live within the law.

If we want people to drive carefully on our roads, observe speed limits, and protect our lives and property, then we must do the same thing for them. It is an act of total selfishness, when one person drives on the roads with disregard to the law, if he complains when involved in an accident with someone else who is also violating the law. When we are under the law, we are protected by the provisions of the law, but if we demand the right of the law, then we are obliged to obey the law ourselves. This principle is an example of genuine justice.

In the Old Testament, David called upon God to deal with his enemies. Perhaps we have thought, 'I wish I could do that! Why could David get away with calling on God to smite his enemies!'? We think, 'Why should people be allowed to cause me all this trouble?' I have come to understand, however, why David could do this. He wrote in one of his psalms:

> *'In your unfailing love, silence my enemies; destroy all my foes, for I am your servant.'*   (Psalm 143:12)

David was being treated unjustly at the time, and under the law was entitled to call to God, for just and legal retribution.

If we demand the right of the law, then we are obliged to obey the law ourselves.

Grace Requires Grace

In Christ, however, we are not under the law, but under grace. We cannot call, as David did, for God to smite our enemy, because David was under the law, and was entitled to the justice of the law. We are not under the law; we are under a provision that is greater and more merciful than the law could ever be! We are now the recipients of God's grace. In simple terms that means that because of what Jesus Christ has done, God sees us through the redemptive work of Christ, and not as we actually are, in ourselves. Grace is the unmerited favour that God shows towards us although we have done nothing to deserve it.

Because we are under grace, we are required to exercise grace in dealing with others. If we want the penalty of the law inflicted on others, then we ourselves come under the same condemnation of the law. The dispensation of grace that we enjoy in Christ gives us so much more, but it requires so much more of us in return. If we are under grace, we cannot make the kind of plea that David made.

There is a new law in operation and that is the law of grace. If I benefit from it, then I am obliged to respond under those same provisions. This is very important, as many of us today want the provisions of God's law to apply to others who have offended us while we in turn want to receive the benefits of grace. We want God to strongly condemn and judge those who have mistreated us, but in turn we want God to treat us kindly! This is a contradiction of the law of grace.

Because we are under grace, we are required to exercise grace in dealing with others.

Forgiveness on a person-to-person basis in the Old Testament was an illustration of grace rather than law. Remember, law was what a person was required to keep and therefore was entitled to demand. As I have mentioned earlier, there are only three illustrations recorded and each one is important, because usually it was a man who called on God for forgiveness. In the Old Testament illustrations, grace was encouraged by God, although He allowed the just provisions of the law. These examples that are given in the Bible pointed toward the higher godlike relationship between people which was to be brought in through Jesus Christ. A new standard of relationship between men and women was to come into operation with the New Covenant: that is the new way that God was prepared to deal with men and women because of what Jesus had done.

Let us examine the three examples we find in the Old Testament regarding person-to-person forgiveness. The first example is found in Genesis chapter 50. We find that Jacob, the father of Joseph, asked Joseph specifically to forgive his brothers for the wrong they had done to him. The message that the brothers brought to Joseph was a direct request from their father. The brothers said, quoting their father:

> *'I ask you to forgive your brothers the sins and wrongs they committed in treating you so badly. Now please forgive the sins of the servants of the God of your father.'*
> (Genesis 50:17)

Here was a request for forgiveness. Joseph's reply was very significant. He said:

> *'Don't be afraid. Am I in the place of God?'*
> (Genesis 50:19)

Joseph realized that although he was not in a position either to judge or pardon, he was being given the privilege of forgiving. Any judgment for the unjust treatment by his brothers was a matter that concerned God, not Joseph!

Notice that the brothers fulfilled the two vital conditions for genuine forgiveness; they acknowledged their sin by confession, and repented of the wrong they had done. On those conditions Joseph forgave them. He declared that although his brothers had meant harm against him, God had used the events for good, and as a result an entire nation had been saved.

Joseph forgave, but the right conditions had been met. It is significant that Joseph said, 'Am I in the place of God?', for he realized that it was not his prerogative to judge or pardon. What God may have done in judging

his brothers the Bible does not tell us. But Joseph, however, had exercised grace towards them, not the provisions of the law.

---

*Joseph realized that although he was not in a
position either to judge or pardon, he was being
given the privilege of forgiving.*

The second example is found in the Bible story of the
deliverance of the Israelites from Egypt. We read these
words of Pharoah:

> 'I have sinned against the Lord your God and against
> you.
> Now forgive my sin once more and pray to the Lord
> your God to take this deadly plague away from me.'
> (Exodus 10:16–17)

Pharoah was ultimately not sincere in that statement,
but it did involve the essential elements of acknowledgment and repentance. We have a man asking for forgiveness, but because he went back on his word, judgment
came upon him.

The third example, a very significant one, is found in
1 Samuel 25. We need to refer to some verses in particular, but a brief outline of the story will help us as this
historical event is important in seeing God's action even
when one man has forgiven another. This incident deals
with the issues of forgiveness and pardon and the continuing judgment when forgiveness has been granted.
There are three major characters in the story: a man
called Nabal, who was a wealthy farmer, the owner of
three thousand sheep and a thousand goats, a woman,

Abigail, Nabal's wife, and David, who was then a fugitive from King Saul.

The Bible record tells us that David's young men had respected and protected Nabal's property, but there came a time when David sent ten of his men to ask for food. This seems to have been a reasonable request in light of the obvious protection that David and his men had given to Nabal. Nabal refused the request, and when the message came back to David, he was angry and set out to take revenge. When Abigail heard what her husband had done, she went out on a mission to intercede for Nabal. The story tells how she rode out to meet David who was coming with the intention of completely destroying all the male members of Nabal's household. She stopped David, apologised, and asked for forgiveness. She had apparently not consulted with her husband, but went on an errand to seek mercy.

This is what Abigail said:

> *'Please forgive your servant's offence, for the Lord will certainly make a lasting dynasty for my master, because he fights the Lord's battles. Let no wrong doing be found in you as long as you live.'*
>
> (1 Samuel 25:28)

David was angry, and obviously felt that he had cause for his anger, but clearly this was a serious over-reaction by David in wanting to take the lives of Nabal's men. He acceded to the request for mercy and forgiveness that Abigail made. He acknowledged that God had directed Abigail in her action, and so was intervening to prevent him from taking an action that he had no right to take — to seek personal revenge.

David said to Abigail:

> *'Praise be to the Lord, the God of Israel, who has sent you today to meet me. May you be blessed for your good judgment and for keeping me from bloodshed this day and from avenging myself with my own hands.'* (1 Samuel 25:32–33)

David realized that the action taken by Abigail was really the intervention of God, stopping him from doing something that would have violated the law of God. David may have tried to justify the action he intended, but he was really seeking to take personal revenge and also to inflict a punishment which was far above the retribution allowed by the law of God. David obviously realized that his intended action would have contravened the principles of God which he relied upon for his own protection.

God was intervening to prevent him from taking an action that he had no right to take – to seek personal revenge.

The story ends in a dramatic way. Abigail returned home and the next day she told her husband what had happened. We read:

> *'Then in the morning, when Nabal was sober, his wife told him all these things, and his heart failed him and he became like a stone. About ten days later, the Lord struck Nabal and he died.'* (1 Samuel 25:37–38)

David had extended both mercy and forgiveness towards Nabal, but the judgment of God on Nabal continued! Nabal had wronged David. David set out to exact retribution to which he was not entitled, but God graciously intervened through Abigail. David saw the error of his intended action, and though he granted the mercy and forgiveness requested by Abigail, David did not have to act in judgment, because it was God who did that! God moved against the ungrateful man Nabal, and he died.

David kept his relationship with God in harmony because of the mercy and forgiveness that he had extended. If David had not forgiven and had instead exacted the vengeance he intended, he may have had an experience similar to that of a later occasion when he took another man's wife and God's judgment came upon him.

We need to recognize that the forgiveness granted by David did not remove God's right to inflict judgment and punishment on the offender.

David kept his fellowship with God in harmony because of the mercy and forgiveness that he had extended.

Choosing Law or Grace

The Old Testament reveals a God of mercy, forgiveness, and pardon. It deals with a people under the law who were obliged to obey the law. It limited personal revenge but allowed just retribution. It allowed a man the privilege of forgiving, but did not demand it from him. It merely demanded just treatment. The Old Testament clearly gave the right to forgive to the individual but, at the same time, showed that God's judgment could still apply to the offender, even when forgiveness had been granted.

The principle we must understand is that if we live under law, then we receive its protection, but we also receive its just penalty. It is strange that born-again believers who are receiving the benefits of God's grace often want to impose the penalties of the law against those who have offended them and they then wonder at the results that follow in their own lives.

Many sincere Christians are determined that believers in Christ should be under a Sabbath Law. It is right to keep a day for God, but if we demand one part of the law, we are obligated to all the law. How amazing that now that we are under grace we should want to be under law. God has set us free through faith in the Lord Jesus Christ, but if we live under grace, then we must also give its provisions to others whom we meet day-by-day. Grace demands a higher response, but it gives greater benefits. We are under grace; we are not under the law! God remains just, righteous, merciful, forgiving, and pardoning, but He requires that the right conditions be met if we are to receive His grace with all its benefits.

How amazing that now we are under grace, we should want to be under law.

It is easy to be judgmental of others and deny them gracious help or restoration, but we can place ourselves in danger by such an attitude.

Immorality is a tragedy and a snare within the church

and especially amongst those in ministry or leadership. I know of a particular incident where the moral failure had been a serious one. The strictest discipline was needed and was exercised. Several years passed before that man was allowed to again take a place on a church platform and preach. The time of discipline had been marked by a complete family reconciliation, a willingness to face the problem, and a spiritual consistency.

When the man concerned was restored to ministry, a fellow minister said, 'A man with that kind of problem should never be allowed back in the ministry!' Within a short time, the minister who had made this judgmental statement was himself exposed for adultery! This man would not then face up to the discipline he had demanded for others.

One of the other errors into which we can fall is to forgive ourselves when forgiveness must first be sought from those whom we have offended. Perhaps in an endeavour to save people from self-condemnation we have stressed the need to forgive ourselves, but this can only properly be done after we have asked others to forgive us for our failure. This means that we have a responsibility to put right any wrongs that we may have committed against another, and not just pretend that the offence did not occur. If we have faithfully done our part in putting right that which was wrong, then we have fulfilled our part even if the other person refuses to accept our request for forgiveness.

As an example I read of a preacher who was scheduled to conduct a series of meetings in a town but suddenly the organizers of the meetings discovered his involvement in a repeated adulterous situation. When confronted with the allegation the man openly confessed his guilt, offered to confess to his wife, and said, 'Now let us get on with the meetings.'

This man had instantly forgiven himself! The organizers cancelled the meetings.

One of the other errors into which we can fall is to forgive ourselves when forgiveness must first come from those whom we have offended.

It is not our right to forgive ourselves, but we must first seek forgiveness from those we have offended. We are not only responsible to God but also to the whole 'Body of Christ'. When appropriate discipline has been applied, and the offender has humbled himself by repentance, then restoration can be set in motion. We have no right to forgive ourselves, until those we have failed offer their forgiveness to us, or we fulfil the conditions that justify such forgiveness. Then we can and should forgive ourselves.

Let me illustrate this from a typical church situation. The youth group had planned an outing, and cars had been arranged to transport all those attending. At the departure time, one car owner had not arrived. The group stood around waiting, a little frustrated and growing anxious as the minutes passed by. Thirty minutes later the missing car with its driver screeched to a halt beside the waiting group, a smiling driver leaning his elbow jauntily on the open window frame. 'Where have you been?' shouted a dozen voices. The young man's grin broadened, 'Better late than never,' he replied self-confidently.

This young man had forgiven himself. His rightful

attitude should have been one of apology and explanation. It was the privilege of the waiting group to forgive him for his late arrival, and no doubt they would have done so had his attitude been right. But he took it as his right to forgive himself. Forgiveness is not obtained in this way.

The opposite attitude is to demand a legalistic approach. The Mosaic law is a great guide to the ways and truth of God, but if we demand its provisions, be prepared to receive them in return. If we want to call God's judgment down on an offender, be prepared for God to bring his judgment down on us. When we appreciate the grace which has been given to us, we will in turn let the grace of God flow out from us, so that in our dealings with each other we will be merciful and forgiving without violating the principle that others must forgive us. Or we must meet the conditions for forgiveness, before we can forgive ourselves.

Some people will hold an attitude of unforgiveness even when a person has apologised and asked to be forgiven, so their wrong response cannot be allowed to be a barrier to our forgiving ourselves. If we follow this course our fellowship with God will be unaffected and we may be sure that a mighty God, who knows all things, is still at work to deal with unrighteousness wherever it might be found. God does not turn 'a blind eye' to the failings, disobedience, and wrongs of Christians, but if they call upon Him in sincerity He will hear and restore them to right relationship with Him. This does not, however, guarantee that God's temporal hand of judgment will not remain upon them. There can be consequences that follow sin, even when forgiveness has been given.

> *God does not turn 'a blind eye' to the failings,*
> *disobedience, and wrongs of Christians, but if*
> *they call on Him in sincerity He will hear and*
> *restore them.*

Let us be sure to show mercy and forgiveness in our
relationships with one another. God can take care of the
offender. It is not our problem, but His! We are to
recognize the grace that we have received through faith
in Jesus Christ, live within the provisions of that grace,
and in return for what we have received, treat others
with grace.

The Lord sent Nathan to David. When he came to him he said, 'There were two men in a certain town, one rich and the other poor.

The rich man had a very large number of sheep and cattle, but the poor man had nothing except one little ewe lamb that he had bought. He raised it and it grew up with him and his children.

It shared his food, drank from his cup and even slept in his arms. It was like a daughter to him.

Now a traveller came to the rich man, but the rich man refrained from taking one of his own sheep or cattle to prepare a meal for the traveller who had come to him. Instead he took the ewe lamb that belonged to the poor man and prepared it for the one who had come to him.'

David burned with anger against the man and said to Nathan, 'As surely as the Lord lives, the man who did this deserves to die.

He must pay for that lamb four times over, because he did such a thing and had no pity.'

Then Nathan said to David, 'You are the man! This is what the Lord, the God of Israel, says: "I anointed you king over Israel, and delivered you from the hand of Saul....

Now, therefore, the sword will never depart from your house, because you despised me and took the wife of Uriah the Hittite to be your own."

'This is what the Lord says: "Out of your own household I am going to bring calamity upon you. Before your very eyes I will take your wives and give them to one who is close to you, and he will lie with your wives in broad daylight.

You did it in secret, but I will do this thing in broad daylight before all Israel."'

Then David said to Nathan, 'I have sinned against the Lord.' Nathan replied, 'The Lord has taken away your sin. You are not going to die.'

(2 Samuel 12:1–7 & 10–13)

Chapter 3

Forgiveness and Judgment

In seeking to understand the proper meaning of forgiveness it is essential, in order to avoid misunderstanding, to realize what happens when forgiveness is given.

It is clear from scripture that the exercise of mercy, which God always grants, and the provision of forgiveness, do not automatically remove all judgment for the offense that has been committed. We need to consider this very carefully as there are implications involved with forgiveness that may have been overlooked. Let me suggest three aspects of forgiveness.

Complete Forgiveness

The term 'complete forgiveness' is used to indicate the total forgiveness of the offender including complete pardon, which removes any continuing judgment for the offense. We read these words in the psalms:

> *'As far as the east is from the west, so far has he removed our transgressions from us.'* (Psalm 103:12)

Jesus made this statement:

> *'This is what is written: "The Christ will suffer and rise from the dead on the third day, and repentance and forgiveness of sins will be preached in his name to all nations, beginning at Jerusalem."'*
>
> (Luke 24:46–47)

In Paul's letter to the Roman church he says:

> *'Blessed are they whose transgressions are forgiven, whose sins are covered.'*
>
> (Romans 4:7)

What marvellous promises these are! It is very plain that there is a forgiveness by God that completely eradicates the penalty of past sin. God can blot out the record of sin so that no consequences remain. This kind of forgiveness restores a person to perfect fellowship with God so that the former sinner, who was alienated from God and without hope, is accepted in Christ just as if he had never committed a sin.

There is a common misconception that God forgets our sins. People say, 'God has cast our sins into the deepest sea of His forgetfulness never to be remembered against us any more.' This statement is not in the Bible although some people may have thought that it was an actual scripture verse! How could an omnipotent, omnipresent, and omniscient God forget? When the Bible refers to God not remembering sins and iniquities it means that God will not act judgmentally against a person or nation, as to penalty or consequences, rather than a literal forgetting that the incident had taken place. An example is as follows:

> *'For I will forgive their wickedness and will remember their sins no more.'*
> (Hebrews 8:12)

God was not going to hold their sin against them, but He had not forgotten that they had sinned! It is easy to use the thought that 'God forgets' as an excuse for not dealing with a problem or not putting right a wrong. When we act in accordance with God's Word, then He puts away the thought of our failure so that it is not a barrier to our relationship with Him. God has the ability not to allow any sin we have committed and then confessed, to affect our fellowship with Him.

There is a forgiveness by God that completely eradicates the penalty of past sin.

This helpful testimony was given to me by a friend:

Early one Sunday morning I found it necesary to correct one of my teenage daughters because of her behaviour. Her response was one of total rejection of what I had said, and I was taken by surprise and offended by her angry reaction.

I did not respond although I felt very annoyed, but went into my room to pray. I had been challenged just previously by the verse in Mark 11:24, *'Therefore I tell you, whatever you ask for in prayer, believe that you have received it, and it will be yours.'*

This scripture was so clear, and here was a need in our home that required God's help, so I asked Him

71

to change my daughter's attitude and give to her the grace of obedience. I asked the Lord to do it that day!

The hours of the day went past with no response from my daughter. At 9.30 p.m. that evening I dropped on my knees beside my bed, and feeling bitterly disappointed I cried out to God and asked Him why He had not answered my prayer. I was certain that I had had the faith to receive that promise.

The next verse in Mark 11 then came to my mind. *'And when you stand praying, if you hold anything against anyone, forgive him, so that your Father in heaven may forgive you your sins.'* I suddenly realized that I was treating forgiveness as forgetting. I had been misled by the cliché, 'God forgives and forgets.' I had put my daughter's remarks and antagonism out of my mind and thought that this constituted forgiveness. My attitude had been passive, just pretending that the incident hadn't taken place, and I was waiting for God to solve the problem. In doing this, I had left my daughter on an island of isolation.

My heart warmed within me and I got up from my knees to go to her room and express my love for her, but God had beaten me to it. My daughter and I met in the passage, each on the way to put things right with the other.

I had thought that trying to forget would solve the problem, but I learnt that day what a vital part forgiveness has in the spiritual realm. As soon as I genuinely forgave from my heart, God moved in her life, and my prayer was answered.

> **It is easy to use the thought that 'God forgets'
> as an excuse for not dealing with a problem or
> not putting right a wrong.**

In a previous chapter we saw the difference between temporal forgiveness and eternal forgiveness. Temporal forgiveness is related to this life whereas eternal forgiveness goes on into eternity. With complete forgiveness, which we are considering now, God also gives total pardon. This means that both in this present life and also eternally, the record is made clear and there are no further penalties for our sins and failures.

How devoid of appreciation we would be if we did not rejoice in a provision such as this! All the guilt and burden of sin are gone. Set free! This is the most common understanding of forgiveness, and it is wonderful to realize that God forgives in such a complete way.

> **Temporal forgiveness is related to this life,
> whereas eternal forgiveness goes on into
> eternity.**

Conditional Forgiveness

We cannot, however, automatically assume that complete forgiveness is always given by God, because there is a second aspect which I will call 'conditional forgiveness'. This is where a person may sin and continue to repeat the offence. God always forgives when the right conditions are met, so it does not matter how serious the failure may be, if the person genuinely repents and confesses, then fellowship with God is restored. Definite conditions are required. God says, 'If you repent and confess, I will restore you to fellowship with me.'

We live in a natural world and are subjected to many pressures and temptations, and we know that yielding to temptation is not always a deliberate or wilful act. There are forces that can gain hold in our lives at different times, and although we have despised ourselves when these sins have occurred, we have failed and repeated a violation of God's Word. It is possible to be entangled by some besetting sin, and many sincere people grapple with this kind of problem. When this happens in our life, God cannot ignore it. God may have to deal with us and place certain restrictions on us as a probation, a proving period to establish discipline and victory in areas of failure. In these circumstances we have the benefit of the Holy Spirit's ministry of convicting us of sin. Jesus said that the Holy Spirit would convict us of sin, righteousness and judgment (John 16:8). We must always be sensitive to this conviction and respond to it if we want the continued blessing of the Lord and also to be free of the consequences that can come from deliberate sin.

God always forgives when the right conditions are met.

At the close of the book of Joshua we read how Joshua warned the people that although God had been with them and had given them victory, the Lord would judge them if they disobeyed His Word or served other gods. These words are recorded:

'Be very strong; be careful to obey all that is written in the Book of the Law of Moses, without turning aside to the right or to the left.

Do not associate with these nations that remain among you; do not invoke the names of their gods or swear by them. You must not serve them or bow down to them.

But you are to hold fast to the Lord your God, as you have until now.

The Lord has driven out before you great and powerful nations; to this day no one has been able to withstand you.

One of you routs a thousand, because the Lord your God fights for you, just as He promised.

So be very careful to love the Lord your God.

But if you turn away and ally yourselves with the survivors of these nations that remain among you and if you intermarry with them and associate with them, then you may be sure that the Lord your God will no longer drive out these nations before you. Instead they will become snares and traps for you, whips on your backs and thorns in your eyes, until you perish from this good land, which the Lord your God has given you.

Now I am about to go the way of all the earth. You know with all your heart and soul that not one of all the good promises the Lord your God gave you has failed. Every promise has been fulfilled; not one has failed.'

(Joshua 23:6–14)

'If you forsake the Lord and serve foreign gods, he will turn and bring disaster on you and make an end of you after he has been good to you.'

(Joshua 24:20)

> **God may have to deal with us and place certain restrictions on us as a probation, a proving period to establish discipline and victory in areas of failure.**

God was warning these people against the consequences of disobedience even after they had enjoyed His supernatural help and blessing.

I wonder whether we take into account the consequences of disobedience in our relationship with God. It was not that they could never be restored again, because God did restore them on many occasions after they violated that particular command, but God warned them of the consequences if they did not do what He said. God was clear! He said that if they did not obey Him and continue in His way, and also completely drive out the enemy, even though He had done so much for them, the Canaanites would recapture the land from them. And it happened!

We could illustrate this from a family situation. It is easy to understand the ways of God if we use the natural family as an example. Think of a child of school age to whom the mother says, 'I want you to come home immediately after school.' The child comes home late and is very apologetic. The mother says, 'All right dear, that's fine, but do not let it happen again.' All is well in the family, the child is forgiven, and the home is in harmony. Next afternoon, the same thing happens, the child is late! Mother says, 'But I told you yesterday to come straight home.' There are tears, more apologies, but repentance restores the happiness of the home. If, however, that conduct continues day after day, then it is inevitable that the mother will place certain restrictions on the child because of the continued disobedience.

The repentance and confession of the child restored fellowship, but the continuation of the offence resulted in discipline being applied. A proving time would be required to work out the full application of forgiveness and again establish a basis for trust. This is how the Holy Spirit works.

Our younger daughter had looked forward eagerly to joining her older brother and sister at school. When she reached the longed-for age of five years, it was an excited little girl who set off for her first day at school. She was cheerful and warm hearted, and quickly made friends. Each afternoon she was a little later in coming home from school. The temptation to spend more time playing with her new friends after school or to stop at a girlfriend's house on the way home was proving too much for her.

My wife told her repeatedly, 'Come home immediately after school.' The little girl's face would look sad and repentant. It was hard for my wife to resist what to us was a cute little blonde whose look could melt the hardest heart, but finally the ultimatum was made, 'You come home immediately after school or else!' But she was late again! 'Where have you been?', demanded my wife. The little head dropped, eyes looked to the ground, and she said, 'I was walking with my head down and I lost my way.'

My wife had to turn away to hide her laughter at the novel excuse from a five year old but, needless to say, for the next few days mother was waiting at the school gate to pick up a little girl who had to learn that 'Come straight home' really meant that! Did we love her less?

Perhaps we even loved her more because of her love of friendship, but discipline had to be taught.

This is the same in our dealings with God. It is perfectly reasonable that our heavenly Father will take restrictive action if we continue to ignore what He says. We expect this to happen in our family. We would not allow a child to go on disobeying but we would not cast out our child from the home or remain with a sullen, angry attitude towards him. If we are mature parents, we would want our relationship with our child restored, but if the child was constantly disobedient, we would be forced to take disciplinary action.

God does this! God sometimes puts restrictions on us, His children, and places us on probation. He puts us through a proving time, to establish that He can really trust us.

I am sure that all of us want God not only to love us but also to trust us. It is true that our human nature often causes us to fall short of the high standard of trustworthiness that God's word portrays, but God is still expecting us to be obedient children. Trying to deceive God is totally unsuccessful, because He knows both our actions and motives. Our children may succeed with deception or disobedience for a time, but with God nothing is hidden. We need a relationship with the Lord where there is not only genuine fellowship through mercy and forgiveness, but also where we are not restricted because He cannot trust us.

Have you ever considered that at a human level there can be genuine love and fellowship without trust? In fact, the Bible tells us that we cannot really trust people, even those who are closest to us. The intentions of people may be worthy but often they fail to live up to those intentions. Our responsibility is to love one another but to trust only God. When we put our trust in people, it is inevitable that at some stage a person will fail that trust, but that does not happen with God.

This idea may at first seem to be contradictory, but careful consideration will show that we can love our children very dearly, and have genuine fellowship with them, but not trust their ability to make right responses in different situations. Because of this, we protect them by discipline and restriction. We do not apply this discipline to harm them, but to save them.

Trying to deceive God is totally unsuccessful, because He knows both our actions and our motives.

If we remember this principle in regard to our relationship with God, it will help to give us better understanding. Our heavenly Father does what we would do with our children, but with much greater understanding, compassion, and love than we could show. There is a conditional forgiveness as well as a complete forgiveness. Conditional forgiveness is where God forgives us of the penalty of the sin, but we are under His restrictive watch. Complete forgiveness is where we are totally restored to God and every sin is wiped out never to be held against us again. We stand before God cleansed from sin and guilt and without restriction because of the blood of Jesus Christ.

If, however, we do not live in obedience but go against the Word of God and please ourselves, God will restore us to fellowship with Him if we repent and confess, but the forgiveness may be conditional.

There are many people today who wonder why certain problems and difficulties happen in their lives. One of the subjects we will deal with is titled 'What is Happening?', because I have had that question asked so often during counselling. People do not understand what is happening in their lives, but if they will accept some of the principles that we are examining, they will begin to understand the cause of many of their problems. God's restrictive, disciplinary hand can be in operation in a person's life, and instead of enjoying complete forgiveness, he is experiencing conditional forgiveness!

God will restore us to fellowship if we repent and confess, but the forgiveness may be conditional.

Judicial Forgiveness

I have called the third aspect of forgiveness 'Judicial Forgiveness'. The laws of the kingdom of God are absolutes. They cannot be broken! We may appear to break them, but we do not, as in reality we break ourselves on God's laws. If we violate these laws, then there is some definite effect upon us.

Always remember that God is merciful, but mercy takes into consideration knowledge and experience, so as we have seen previously, the degree of mercy that is extended varies according to the knowledge and understanding that a person has. If a new Christian commits a sin, then God's mercy toward him may be much greater than if an experienced Christian committed the same sin.

Mercy is the lessening of the severity of the penalty which is deserved. We read in James' letter:

> *'Dear brothers, don't be too eager to tell others their faults, for we all make many mistakes; and when we teachers, who should know better, do wrong, our punishment will be greater than it would be for others.'*
>
> (James 3:1 The Living Bible)

This truth of repentance and judicial forgiveness is clearly illustrated in two examples from the life of King David. I want to examine these because they are very important in giving us clarity in all aspects of forgiveness. The scripture states:

> *'So the king said to Joab and the army commanders with him, "Go throughout the tribes of Israel from Dan to Beersheba and enrol the fighting men, so that I may know how many there are."*
> *But Joab replied to the king, "May the Lord your God multiply the troops a hundred times over, and may the eyes of my lord the king see it. But why does my lord the king want to do such a thing?"*
> *The king's word, however, overruled Joab and the army commanders; so they left the presence of the king to enrol the fighting men of Israel.'*
>
> (2 Samuel 24:2–4)

The story continues in the same chapter:

> *'David was conscience-stricken after he had counted the fighting men, and he said to the Lord, "I have sinned greatly in what I have done. Now O Lord, I beg you, take away the guilt of your servant. I have done a very foolish thing."'*
> (2 Samuel 24:10)

This was a clear statement of repentance and confession by David. God, however, sent the prophet Gad, David's seer, to David. This is what the Bible records:

> *'Go and tell David, "This is what the Lord says: I am giving you three options. Choose one of them for me to carry out against you."*
> *So Gad went to David and said to him, "Shall there come upon you three years of famine in your land? Or three months of fleeing from your enemies while they pursue you? Or three days of plague in your land? Now then, think it over and decide how I should answer the one who sent me."*
> *David said to Gad, "I am in deep distress. Let us fall into the hands of the Lord, for his mercy is great; but do not let me fall into the hands of men."*
> *So the Lord sent a plague on Israel from that morning until the end of the time designated, and seventy thousand of the people fron Dan to Beersheba died.'*
>
> (2 Samuel 24:12–15)

Some offences in the sight of God are so serious that although God will forgive if there is repentance and confession, there is a continuing judicial result.

David had repented and confessed his sin, but God still sent judgment! The full implications of David's action in numbering the people is not clear in the scripture. There is a proviso made in the Old Testament for numbering the people, but it would seem, because of the penalty which God imposed, that behind David's action in numbering the people was pride in what he had achieved. It would appear that David must have had self-satisfaction because of the number of people he had gathered around him. David had failed to acknowledge that it was God who had given him power and victory.

David's generals, Joab and others, had pleaded with him not to number the people, but he had gone ahead wilfully. Now, realizing the enormity of his action, he cried out to God in repentance. But it was too late!

David was restored to fellowship with God as a result of his repentance, but pardon for the consequences of his sin was not granted. Because of David's action, judgment fell on the whole nation. There was a continuing judicial result from David's failure.

Perhaps this should be a salutory lesson for some Christian leaders today who put great stress on the numbers of people who attend their meetings. We need to constantly remember that any success that we enjoy is because of God's grace and His Spirit rather than on our own energies or abilities.

A more serious illustration is the one dealing with David's adultery with Bathsheba, and the arranged death of her husband, Uriah. These undoubtedly were the darkest events in David's life. The story is recorded in 2 Samuel 11. Later David was confronted with these two sins, his adultery, and the murder of one of the men who had trusted him.

Some commentators say that it may have been up to four years before David genuinely repented and asked God's forgiveness even though David did immediately recognize what he had done, but was unwilling to face up to his actions. We can accept that we have done wrong but not genuinely repent. David instantly acknowledged his sin, but could not have been genuinely repentant, because he was not immediately restored to fellowship with God (Psalm 32:3–4). If we want to understand the inner battle that David experienced in seeking to be restored in his relationship with the Lord, we can read his own account in Psalm 32. This psalm reveals a period of great personal struggle before David finally and sincerely confessed and repented of the enormity of his sin. The Living Bible paraphrases the experience of David in this graphic manner:

> '*What happiness for those whose guilt has been forgiven!*
> *What joys when sins are covered over! What relief for those who have confessed their sins and God has cleared their record.*
> *There was a time when I wouldn't admit what a sinner I was. But my dishonesty made me miserable and filled my days with frustration. All day and all night your hand was heavy on me. My strength evaporated like water on a sunny day until I finally admitted my sins to you and stopped trying to hide them. I said to myself, "I will confess them to the Lord." And you forgave me! All my guilt is gone.*'   (Psalm 32:1–5)

We can recognize that we have done wrong but not genuinely repent.

What a dramatic account of an inner conflict. David finally reached the place of genuine sorrow. He repented, and confessed, and God restored him to fellowship with Him. One cannot read Psalm 32 without sensing the great weight that had been lifted from David and the joy that was now within him even though discipline and judgment were not removed. This is confirmed as we read David's words in Psalm 51. David was obviously aware of the continuing effect his sin had on God's highest purpose for his life. It is sobering to read the verses of this psalm again in the light of what has been presented in this study:

> 'Have mercy upon me, O God, according to your unfailing love; according to your great compassion blot out my transgression.
> Wash away all my iniquity and cleanse me from my sin.
> For I know my transgressions, and my sin is always before me.
> Against you, you only, have I sinned and done what is evil in your sight, so that you are proved right when you speak and justified when you judge.'
>
> (Psalm 51:1–4)

> 'Hide your face from my sins and blot out all my iniquity.
> Create in me a pure heart, O God, and renew a steadfast spirit within me.
> Do not cast me from your presence or take your Holy Spirit from me.
> Restore to me the joy of your salvation and grant me a willing spirit, to sustain me.
> Then I will teach transgressors your ways, and sinners will turn back to you.'   (Psalm 51:9–13)

> 'You do not delight in sacrifice, or I would bring it; you do not take pleasure in burnt offerings.
> The sacrifices of God are a broken spirit; a broken and contrite heart, O God you will not despise.'
>
> (Psalm 51: 16–17)

Continuing Judgment

Many Christians have been unwilling to face the fact that there can be continuing judgment after forgiveness has been given. It is easy to say, *'As far as the east is from the west, so far has He removed our transgressions from us'* (Psalm 103:12). We can take that to mean that our sin is blotted out and finished with in every way, but that may not be correct. I have heard people say when they speak about the mercy and forgiveness of God, 'Well, love covers a multitude of sins, God is a loving God, and will not hold our failure against us.'

Many Christians have been unwilling to face the fact that there can be continuing judgment after forgiveness has been given.

If we are seeking to grow spiritually, we need to take this aspect to heart. In David's case, God's forgiveness did not eliminate the consequences of an action. Not only did the child that was born to Bathsheba die, but God inflicted a continuing temporal judgment on David. He was told by the prophet Nathan:

> *'Now, therefore, the sword shall never depart from your house, because you despised me and took the wife of Uriah the Hittite to be your own.'*
>
> (2 Samuel 12:10)

These words were spoken to David who was described as 'a man after God's own heart!' David had been chosen by God and ordained to be king of Israel. He loved to praise and worship the Lord and to have fellowship with Him. David, however, was a man who had become captured by lust for Bathsheba. He finally repented, but although God forgave him for the sins he had committed, death and trouble continued to inflict his family. There was continued temporal consequences of his sin. Disasters and heartache followed David's family.

Ammon, David's son, raped his own sister, and later paid the penalty with his life. Absalom plotted against his father to take the throne and won the hearts of the people by deceit. David suffered betrayal by Absalom, and later Absalom died violently. In spite of Absalom's deception, David was in great distress when told of his son's death. We read in the scripture record:

> *'The king was shaken. He went up to the room over the gateway and wept. As he went he said: "O my son Absalom! My son, my son Absalom! If only I had died instead of you – O Absalom, my son, my son!"'*
>
> (2 Samuel 18:33)

We would have hard hearts if we did not feel something of this father's anguish. Even the great and wise Solomon who succeeded his father David as king of Israel, ended his days in selfish pleasure, his heart turned away from God. David's household did suffer because of his sins.

We live today in a permissive society where adultery and fornication have become commonplace. I think it is sobering to remember that under the law of Moses adultery received the penalty of death by stoning. God particularly said to David, *'You are not going to die'* (2 Samuel 12:13).

David should have died under the terms of the law but God, however, showed mercy upon him and did not demand the full penalty of the law. However, the consequences of David's sin continued to affect him and his family.

Law or Principle?

I suppose some people would say, 'Isn't that only Old Testament punishment?' This would leave us with the question to answer as to whether we are dealing with an Old Testament story or with a principle of God. If it is a principle of God, then it does not change.

In 1 John 5:16 the apostle John writes about a sin that is not unto death and a sin that is unto death. In Matthew Henry's Bible Commentary on this particular verse he says:

> 'The gospel does not positively threaten death for the more visible sins of the members of Christ, but only some chastisement. There is room left for divine wisdom or goodness or even severity, to determine how far the chastisement or the scourge shall proceed.'

The consequences of David's sin continued to affect him and his family.

There is also a New Testament pattern for the continuing dealings of God as to consequences, even when fellowship has been restored to God through mercy and forgiveness. An example of a temporal or earthly judgment proceeding, even though there has been prior forgiveness, is found in Hebrews 6. This chapter begins with statements of the great foundational doctrines of our faith and goes on to make this declaration:

> *'It is impossible for those who have once been enlightened, who have tasted the heavenly gift, who have shared in the Holy Spirit, who have tasted the goodness of the word of God and the powers of the coming age, if they shall fall away, to be brought back to repentance, because to their loss they are crucifying the Son of God all over again and subjecting him to public disgrace.'*
>
> (Hebrews 6:4–6)

This is a very solemn passage of scripture. God's purpose toward us is good, but in the midst of our joy in the blessings He gives, we also need to understand the principles by which we grow to full maturity. The Christians referred to in Hebrews 6 obviously had experienced a deep relationship with God. They had been enlightened and had tasted the heavenly gift. They had shared in the work of the Holy Spirit. If, however, after all of this they fell away from their faith, the scripture is very final; it is impossible to bring them back to repentance!

Does this mean a loss of salvation? Salvation is not lost because of some failure or indiscretion although it is possible for one to lose his salvation. Eternal security comes from a continuing relationship with Jesus Christ, so we need to be careful in seeking to understand this particular part of God's Word.

Perhaps, when God has blessed us with His goodness, has filled us with the Holy Spirit, and has given gifts of the Spirit, and we repudiate these by word or action, it becomes impossible to bring us back to the same place of relationship with the Lord. I have seen this happen to people! They have never been restored to a vital place in God, after denying or treating lightly a powerful experience of God's grace and power.

There are, however, those who would place a much stricter interpretation on these verses. They would see these scriptures as referring to a person who has had a deep personal experience of God and then deliberately and completely turns his back on the Lord and the truth of the Bible. This would be interpreted as a 'sin unto death' from which there is no place of restoration. No doubt this can happen, but in general, this scripture possibly refers to a continuing temporal judgment rather than loss of salvation.

There are dealings of God that begin in this present life, and even if there is genuine confession and repentance, there is no way that we are able to escape the judicial hand of God.

The story of Esau is another example. It would seem, that when he sold his birthright to his brother Jacob for the price of a meal, that he did so without considering all the implications of his action. The writer to the Hebrews, refers to this incident and says:

> *'See that no-one is sexually immoral, or is godless like Esau, who for a single meal sold his inheritance rights as the oldest son. Afterwards, as you know, when he wanted to inherit this blessing, he was rejected. He could bring about no change of mind, though he sought the blessing with tears.'*
>
> (Hebrews 12:16–17)

This is another illustration of apparent repentance where the loss which had been suffered could not be restored. We need to consider the consequences before embarking on a course of action that violates the principles of God.

> *Even if there is genuine confession and repentance, there is no way that we are able to escape the judicial hand of God.*

Facing Failure

What is the answer to a situation such as this? There is only one remedy. If we have gone against the Word of God to the extent that the judicial hand of God remains on us, after we have repented and asked to be forgiven, then the only answer is to humble ourselves before the Lord. Face the problem. Don't excuse it. Accept it. Look it straight in the face and say, 'Yes, it happened, and I am responsible.'

In humbling ourselves before the Lord, we must admit what we have done. We must then allow God's actions in our lives without resistance. The more we resist, if we are under the judicial dealings of God, the longer we will remain there. It is only when we say, 'Lord, I am desperately in need of your mercy, forgiveness and pardon' that we open the way for God to lift his judgment and discipline. Like David of old, we must say, 'I will throw myself upon the mercy of God.' Then stay close to the Lord.

It is hard to face failure, or acknowledge that we may have been wrong. Very few people ever have the courage to retrace their steps. I have known many people who have, for various reasons, been upset over some aspect of church life or emphasis and have left the church, usually with the comment that the Lord had directed them in their action.

Many of these people have subsequently become spiritual wanderers and their Christian growth has become stunted, clearly indicating by the fruit of their lives that their original decision to leave the church was not at God's direction.

I well remember a young man who influenced a group of young people to become discontented and critical and leave the church where I pastored. The accusation levelled at the ministry was that there was a lack of faith preaching. This young man declared that if one had sufficient faith, one could have anything one wanted. The young man concerned left the Teachers College where he was training and declared that the Lord had told him to read the Bible and wait on Him.

For some weeks the friends of the young man rallied around him, paying the rent of his apartment and providing money for his food, until they became disillusioned by the events. Ultimately the young man applied to go back to University, and as far as I know, his spiritual involvement in active church life came to a standstill. He never came back to apologize for his accusations or the upset caused in many other lives.

It is hard to be humble enough to ask for forgiveness when we have thought that we were right but found that we were wrong. Most people just try to forget about it or pretend that nothing serious happened. It is true that many of our errors begin out of sincerity but the ministry of the Holy Spirit is to guide us into truth, so if we will keep a teachable spirit we will soon come under conviction. The sad part is that so many people will not take steps to put right what is wrong.

Sin does not have to be some serious immoral action as any kind of disobedience or self-will can make it necessary for us to humble ourselves in order to be restored to the right place of fellowship that God wants us to have with Him.

It is significant that when Achan disobeyed God's command and the nation of Israel suffered defeat at the city of Ai, the people had to go back to the place of defeat and conquer that city before they could proceed any further in their conquest of the Promised Land of Canaan. This is a good illustration of how we must go back to the place of defeat and deal with the failure if we are to grow in our spiritual lives.

It is hard to be humble enough to ask for forgiveness when we have thought that we were right but found that we were wrong.

Three Kinds of Judgment

Judgment can be a part of genuine forgiveness! There are three kinds of judgment that apply:

1. Self-judgment

'Therefore let us stop passing judgment on one another. Instead, make up your mind not to put any stumbling block or obstacle in your brother's way.'
(Romans 14:13)

This verse tells us that we are to judge our own actions. In his letter to the Corinthian church the apostle Paul was teaching about the manner in which believers were to come to the Lord's table, and he said:

'A man ought to examine himself before he eats of the bread and drinks of the cup.'   (1 Corinthians 11:28)

The Lord requires a genuine honest self-examination. To quote further from the same chapter of Paul's letter:

'But if we judged ourselves, we would not come under judgment. When we are judged by the Lord, we are being disciplined so that we will not be condemned with the world.' (1 Corinthians 11:31–32)

This teaching is clear; if we are willing to judge ourselves, then God's judgment does not come on us, but if we do not judge ourselves, then God will judge us and bring on us whatever discipline is needed.

2. Judgment by the Church

This might be a new aspect to some, because we seldom do this in practice. Jesus was, however, very clear about it and gave specific instructions about the procedure to be followed when there was a dispute between believers:

'If your brother sins against you, go and show him his fault, just between the two of you. If he listens to you, you have won your brother over. But if he will not listen, take one or two others along, so that "every matter may be established by the testimony of two or three witnesses." If he refuses to listen to them, tell it to the church; and if he refuses to listen even to the church, treat him as you would a pagan or a tax collector.' (Matthew 18:15–17)

In 1 Corinthians 5, there is another reference to judging the wrong conduct of believers. We are told not to keep company with any man who calls himself a brother but is sexually immoral or greedy, an idolator or a slanderer, a drunkard or a swindler.

These are strong words, but they are clear instructions

to those in the church as to how they are to act toward others who say they are believers but are guilty of bad behaviour. In Paul's letter to Titus we read the following:

'For there are many rebellious people, mere talkers and deceivers, especially those of the circumcision group. They must be silenced, because they are ruining whole households by teaching things they ought not to teach – and that for the sake of dishonest gain. Even one of their own prophets has said, "Cretans are always liars, evil brutes, lazy gluttons." This testimony is true. Therefore rebuke them sharply, so that they will be sound in the faith.' (Titus 1:10–13)

The rebuke and penalty are not for the purpose of ridding the church of undesirable people, but to discipline them in the Christian faith. The church has a powerful judicial authority under God. Generally speaking, we have failed to exercise this responsibility, but it is provided for in scripture.

3. The judgment of God Himself

We have seen by the illustrations that have been given that God's dealings can continue even after forgiveness has been granted. We read this in Hebrews:

'For we know him who said, "It is mine to avenge; I will repay," and again, "The Lord will judge his people." It is a dreadful thing to fall into the hands of the living God.' (Hebrews 10:30–31)

This warning is written to Christians! If we wish to escape from the judicial hand of God, it is not only a matter of receiving His mercy and forgiveness, but we must also humble ourselves by allowing judgment, through the conviction of the Holy Spirit or admonition of other Christians. We must also be open, if necessary, for judgment by the church, always recognizing that unless we do so, the judgment of God upon us will continue.

The church has a powerful judicial authority under God.

What has been said in the preceding paragraph must be emphasized, because it is always God's desire to restore people to right relationship with one another and also with Him.

The apostle Paul taught clearly that there was to be restoration after judgment. I am glad we have a God like this because who of us would want to punish our child week after week or month after month? Punishment of a child may be necessary because of a rebellious attitude, disobedience, or carelessness, but I am sure that loving people would want restoration. God does not want to be always inflicting discipline. God does not want to have His family under a heavy hand of judgment! His desire is that we should walk in joyous fellowship with Him. We can do that by living in the light of God's Word.

Restoration after Judgment

Consider two passages in the letter to the Corinthians:

> *'It is actually reported that there is sexual immorality among you, and of a kind that does not occur even among pagans: A man has his father's wife.*

*And you are proud! Shouldn't you rather have been
filled with grief and have put out of your fellowship
the man who did this?*
*Even though I am not physically present, I am with
you in spirit. And I have already passed judgment on
the one who did this, just as if I were present.*
*When you are assembled in the name of our Lord
Jesus and I am with you in spirit, and the power of
our Lord Jesus is present, hand this man over to
Satan, so that the sinful nature may be destroyed and
his spirit saved on the day of the Lord.'*

(1 Corinthians 5:1–5)

This scripture tells of the disciplinary action against a
man who was immoral, but a member of the church. The
instruction was to deliver him to Satan, for the destruction of his flesh. When we come to Paul's second letter to
the Corinthian church we find, however, that Paul is
urging restoration for this man:

*'The punishment inflicted on him by the majority is
sufficient for him. Now instead, you ought to forgive
and comfort him, so that he will not be overwhelmed
by excessive sorrow. I urge you, therefore, to reaffirm
your love for him.'*

(2 Corinthians 2:6–8)

We now see the church members being encouraged to
restore the one who had sinned, and to comfort and love
him. There is a need for us to be totally honest in applying the principles of God's Word. If we want genuine
forgiveness, let us realize that much more is involved
than just ignoring the sin that has been committed.

The church has a reputation for killing off its
wounded! One of the greatest blessings we can receive is

to see a person who has failed being fully restored. I remember hearing this quote, 'We are not failures because we fail; we are only failures when we stop trying.'

The Bible is a book of restoration. I know many people who have failed badly in their personal lives, but I have also seen some of them humble themselves, take the appropriate discipline which was given, maintain a humble and repentant attitude, and be fully restored to positions of responsibility and blessing.

If we want genuine forgiveness, let us realize that more is involved than ignoring the sin that has been committed.

God is merciful and forgiving, but it is possible to remain under His judgment although our relationship with Him has been restored. God's desire, however, is not only to restore us to fellowship with Him but also that we might enjoy the benefits of full pardon through the discipline we receive. When sin is acknowledged and discipline accepted, then the conditions have been established for full restoration to take place.

Judgment and discipline are essential conditions before the full provisions of forgiveness and pardon are enjoyed by the Christian who has wilfully sinned.

'If your brother sins against you, go and show him his fault, just between the two of you. If he listens to you, you have won your brother over.

But if he will not listen, take one or two others along, so that "every matter may be established by the testimony of two or three witnesses."

If he refuses to listen to them, tell it to the church; and if he refuses to listen even to the church, treat him as you would a pagan or a tax collector ....

Then Peter came to Jesus and asked, "Lord, how many times shall I forgive my brother when he sins against me? Up to seven times?"

Jesus answered, "I tell you, not seven times, but seventy-seven times."'   (Matthew 18:15–17 & 21–22)

Chapter 4

Forgiveness in The New Testament

We come now to the words of the Master Teacher Himself, the Lord Jesus Christ.

Forgiven As We Forgive?

What Jesus taught is found in the Sermon on the Mount, Matthew 5–7, and also in the different parables He told. We have shown in the course of this study that God is forgiving. There is no question about that! We do have a wonderful God who forgives, but it is possible for certain consequences to continue even after we have been forgiven. The way to deal with these consequences is by humbling ourselves, judging ourselves, allowing the judgment of the church as provided for in scripture if that is necessary, and recognizing God's right to judge and discipline us through the direction of the Holy Spirit. Some consequences may continue, but by meeting the biblical requirements we can lessen the penalties which otherwise might apply.

Our Heavenly Father has a right to exercise a disciplinary hand upon those who belong to His family, so even after God has restored us to fellowship with Him,

He may continue to take restrictive action against us until such time as we have proved ourselves by obedience to His Word. God alone is the judge of this, so we must maintain a submissive attitude at all times.

Perhaps the most challenging aspect of this subject is the application of forgiveness between individuals. As Christians we are called upon to forgive others, so the question arises concerning the effect that our forgiving or failure to forgive has upon God's forgiveness of us. In other words, to what extent does our response to the command to forgive others reflect on the forgiveness we receive from God?

There are some important comparative scriptures that need to be examined. The first is found in the Sermon on the Mount, where Jesus said:

> *'For if you forgive men when they sin against you, your heavenly Father will also forgive you.*
> *But if you do not forgive men their sins, your Father will not forgive your sins.'*　　(Matthew 6:14–15)

This is a very strong statement by Jesus and we need to understand the full implication of these words. The second reference is found in Mark's gospel:

> *'And when you stand praying, if you hold anything against anyone, forgive him, so that your Father in heaven may forgive you your sins.'*　(Mark 11:25–26)

The third reference is found in Luke's gospel:

> *'Forgive us our sins, for we also forgive everyone who sins against us. And lead us not into temptation.'*
> 　　　　　　　　　　　　　　　　　　(Luke 11:4)

There are many people who misunderstand these scriptures, and read into them an obligation that they often find impossible to fulfil. This leads them either into condemnation or pretence. There is a depth of meaning in these verses that we must understand in order to find a clear answer. A casual reading of these passages could leave a person thinking that he would be forgiven by God only to the extent that he was willing or able to forgive another. That is true in a certain aspect but it must be qualified.

There are also those people who gain a certain spiritual satisfaction from forgiving others for their failures but never look at their own bad behaviour or realise that most of the difficulties begin with them and not with those they are anxious to forgive! This will be discussed in the next chapter.

Grace or Works?

If our concept of forgiveness includes the provision of pardon, then the question would immediately arise as to who would be saved if our salvation depended upon the extent to which we from the heart forgave others? Was Jesus dealing with the question of the forgiveness that relates to salvation, and which includes pardon, or some other aspect of forgiveness?

Over many years of counselling, I have found that people have deep hurts and problems in their lives related to the issues of forgiveness and unforgiveness. Most of them have been committed Christians and many were baptized with the Holy Spirit and were active in church life. They loved God, and yet they made such statements as this; 'I have been so hurt and

wounded emotionally and mentally that I find it impossible to forgive.' The hurt may have been caused by a
parent, or someone else close to them, and they were
unable to forgive that person.

**Who would be saved if our salvation depended
upon the extent to which we from the heart
forgave others?**

Was I dealing with a person who was outside of the
salvation of Christ, because Jesus said that if we do not
forgive one another then our Heavenly Father will not
forgive us? Let me include another illustration from my
personal experience.

Before becoming Christians, a husband and wife had
experienced a stormy and largely unhappy marriage.
There were constant confrontations and angry words
that had left bitter hurts. When they accepted Christ, a
new love and understanding developed but problems
remained over matters of money and other frustrations
that had also arisen in their relationship.

I spent many hours with them in counselling and
advice on budgeting and in other areas where difficulties
occurred, and although these matters seemed to become
resolved, it was never long before another crisis arose.
There are always two sides to any story, but I had no
doubt that the major problems occurred because of the
husband's demanding and obstinate attitude. He developed some deviant ways which added to the pressures in
the home, and in desperation the wife left the house in
the hope that a trial separation might help solve the
problems.

We continued the counselling, and I appointed others

to take a more detailed oversight, but although the husband showed repentance, it was not long before his old ways and attitudes returned. Separation and reconciliation occurred again and again with the wife wanting to do the right thing, but finding that conditions always became intolerable. Finally she could take no more! Some serious events had taken place in the husband's conduct that made it impossible for me to insist that the wife should return to her husband, and as she had tried so often before, she had now reached the end of her ability to forgive and be reconciled.

The husband continued to demand reconciliation, but the wife could not face the prospect of again going through the emotionally destroying experiences that she had suffered so often before. The husband sued for divorce. Some Christians would ask whether the woman had endangered her salvation? The answer to this question is no. The woman's refusal to return to her husband did not endanger her salvation, but her refusal to forgive her husband could lead to other problems which would reduce her spiritual effectiveness.

Many people live with guilt and are under condemnation because they cannot forgive. The hurts they have suffered are genuine. They may have been greatly wronged; perhaps someone had taken advantage of them when they were children. Serious cases of child abuse are now regularly being exposed. Marriages may have broken down, or friends may have betrayed the trust put in them. People have been in a position emotionally where they have been so hurt that they did not know how to forgive. As a result they have been under a great sense of guilt and fear. With many such people there is also a deep inner bitterness.

The Bible warns that we must be careful lest a root of bitterness springs up and defiles us, and unforgiveness is the cause of this root of bitterness. It can cloud reality, distort thinking, and lead to severe emotional instability. Deep within these people who wanted to love and serve God were hurts that created anger, fear, resentment, and guilt. Unresolved pain and unforgiveness can lead to doubts as to whether they were in right relationship with God in regard to their salvation.

Many people live with guilt and under condemnation because they cannot forgive.

Prior to the divorce proceedings of the aforementioned couple, many vindictive actions had been taken by the husband towards his estranged wife. Facts were distorted and information was given to other people who should not have been involved. The wife was deeply hurt, and I can understand how hard it must have been for her to face false accusations. It is easy to sit in an Ivory Tower and demand what should be done in particular circumstances, but when one is in the midst of a problem like this, it is extremely difficult to genuinely forgive. The home life was ruined!

All this time, the woman had maintained her church fellowship and I have no doubt that her eternal salvation was secure, in spite of the tremendous inner battle she was enduring. I now quote from a written testimony which she gave to me:

'Forgive your husband.' The words seemed so clear although there was no audible voice. It was a time when I was seeking the Lord for an answer to false

106

accusations being made against me. I had lost some of my joy and peace but did not think that I had been harbouring unforgiveness in my heart towards my former husband.

The words rang through my mind and I felt an inner shock. I suddenly realized that I had been sinning against God and I asked for His forgiveness. Then I said to the Lord that I would sincerely forgive my husband, but I knew that I would also need to go and see him and put matters right. I acted quickly and went to see him. Not only did he receive my confession and expression of forgiveness, but we exchanged mutual forgiveness and love and peace towards each other which only the Holy Spirit could have made possible.

I instantly found a new sense of God's love and His joy and peace.

I would have liked to have been able to say that this marriage was saved and restored, but that did not occur. The second best took place and the two people found a place of sincere forgiveness of each other although they could not face the prospect of continuing with their marriage. God hates divorce, but sometimes every effort seems to fail in getting diverse people to live in harmony and we have to accept the reality of separation. I do not believe that this failure is due to the lack of power that the Lord provides, but is due to our human inability to appropriate the fulness of what is provided through the Holy Spirit.

In counselling with people who have gone through marriage problems similar to this, I agree that situations can become so ugly when one party does not want to change, that the other party has no option but to finally get out of the marriage for his or her own sanity and health. There are times when the scripture tells us to *'Shake the dust off your feet'* (Matthew 10:14). We must, however, genuinely try, and try hard, before we resort to an action that is essentially against that which God desires.

I am not prepared to say that a problem is hopeless. I believe in the power of hope and consider that we should hold to our hopes even in the most difficult circumstances, until we are absolutely sure that the door to a particular hope has been finally closed. Then we must allow the Holy Spirit to put new hope back into our hearts and minds and press forward in our lives, and in the fulfilment of God's plan for us.

The difficulty in genuinely forgiving is a very real dilemma that is faced by many people, and they have been afraid to speak about it. I have discovered that many people go through serious crises in their spiritual lives, but are afraid to talk about problems as they feel they are the only ones with the particular problem. By sharing their difficulty with someone else they feel inferior as Christians, and Satan delights in deceiving sincere believers in such a manner. We all face these challenges and need to understand how they can be combated and overcome. To do this we must understand the real meaning of forgiveness and what is involved when we forgive. Let us consider these points.

If our salvation is dependent upon our ability to completely forgive others from the heart, then the salvation of many born again and Spirit-filled Christians would be in doubt, because unforgiveness is, without question, a problem in the church.

If our salvation depends on our ability to completely

forgive others from the heart, then where does the Bible truth of justification by faith stand?

Are we justified by our faith in Christ plus our ability to forgive another person or are we justified before a holy God because of the provisions of Calvary and the blood of Jesus Christ alone? The Word of God tells us that we are saved by grace through faith, an act of repentance and confession of our sin, not because of an ability to forgive another who may have seriously wronged us.

The Need to Forgive

In saying these things, we are not for one moment minimizing the need to forgive one another, but we are putting the Bible teaching concerning forgiveness into a right perspective. It needs to be strongly emphasized that we are now referring to the question of forgiving one another only in regard to how it affects our salvation.

Salvation is an act of mercy by a loving God which incorporates His mercy, forgiveness, and pardon. The benefits of salvation are bestowed upon us as a result of grace, and grace alone. Our salvation, therefore, is not dependent upon our ability to forgive another person who has wronged us, but is dependent entirely on the grace of God and the response of our hearts in repentance and confession.

We are saved by grace through faith, by an act of repentance and confession of our sin, not because of an ability to forgive another who may have seriously wronged us.

I am not condoning unforgiveness! Jesus taught that we must forgive one another. There is a desperate need for individual Christians to learn to forgive one another. Many people are in serious turmoil spiritually, mentally, emotionally, and physically, because they have been unwilling to forgive. The hurts they have suffered have been so deep that they say they are unable to forgive. Mostly, this inability is due to unwillingness to forgive, but other times it is due to not knowing how to begin to forgive. The task is too great for them and they do not know that showing mercy is the first step to forgiveness.

Perhaps, because of unforgiveness, a demonic spirit has gained a hold so that the person finds he is powerless in the battle to become willing to forgive. His will to genuinely forgive has become so gripped by Satan's power, that he fails to do what he knows should be done. A person in this condition may need special prayer for deliverance.

We are not condoning unforgiveness! Jesus taught that we must forgive one another.

Generally speaking, however, all unforgiveness is due, at least in the first instance, to an unwillingness or ignorance of how to forgive. None of us can say that we are unable to forgive, because the Word of God tells us that we are to forgive. It would be a contradiction in terms to say that the Bible tells us to forgive but that really it is impossible to do so. If the Bible declares that we are to forgive one another, then obviously this is what we should do and what we are able to do if we know the steps. Forgiveness has to do with heart attitude. We

110

have already said that forgiveness involves the dismissal of resentment or displeasure.

I was given this personal testimony:

> My childhood was mainly unhappy because of the constant arguing of my father and mother. It was not until my early teens that I began to realize the great pressure that my mother suffered because of the heavy drinking habits of my father and his infidelity with other women. I loved my father and there were some happy family times, but they were short-lived. In my mid-teens, my father left home to live with another woman and an added financial strain was placed upon our family.
>
> As I grew older and married, I just wanted to put my father out of my mind altogether, and I had no desire to see him again. I thought that 'forgetting' would solve the problem of the deep hurt I had suffered because of a broken home. The years passed by but I did not realize that there was really a deep unforgiveness and bitterness still existing within me towards my father. During this time, God was blessing our lives and my husband and I had come into new experiences of God's provision and empowering.
>
> A telephone call shattered my life! My brother whom I loved dearly had been killed in an accident. My husband and I flew the long distance back to my home-city for the funeral. As I stepped from the aircraft, the first person I saw was my father. My emotions were in turmoil, but we embraced and something happened inside me. My father was a broken man – devastated by the death of the son he

had mainly neglected – and I felt compassion and forgiveness welling up within me.

We were able to visit him later and I found all my old hurts and displeasure were gone. Sorrow and disappointment remained, but I found a new peace and contentment. I discovered that trying to forget was very different from forgiving.

Do We Deserve Forgiveness?

There are practical ways to overcome the problem of forgiving others. We must face up to the fact that we did not deserve anything from God ourselves, except judgment, but He forgave us. He also went beyond forgiveness and pardoned us as well. He took away the guilt and penalty of our sins so we are debtors to the mercy and grace of God. Everyone who has made a commitment of his life to Jesus Christ is a debtor to the grace, mercy, and forgiveness of God. If God forgave us a debt beyond our ability to pay, then it is a comparatively small thing for us to forgive another some trespass against us, because any wrong that is done to us could never compare with the wrong that we have done to God.

That may be hard for a person to accept when they are hurting! We feel our own hurts very deeply and our human minds can be very self-centred. This is why the Bible stresses the need for the mind to be renewed and protected, otherwise our feelings will distort our ability to objectively accept the truth of what the Bible says.

It was our sin that made the sacrifice of Christ necessary. It was the sin of mankind, and the sin that we have committed, that made it necessary for Christ to be separated from His Father and suffer and die. The hurts that we have suffered from others are so small compared to the enormity of our sin against God. When we think about this objectively we know it is true, but it is hard to view our circumstances objectively when we are in distress. It is only after we have begun to heal and get hold of life again that we realize the enormity of our sin against God, others and ourselves. We sin against ourselves when we revel in pain and we sin against our Creator when we do not allow Him to heal us and guide us into wholeness in spirit, soul, and body.

We need to come to a practical realization of the effects of our sins toward others and toward God, because it will help us to forgive the transgressions of others against us. In the parable of the Unmerciful Servant, which we have already referred to and which is found in Matthew 18, this principle is very clearly shown. The truths contained in this story are so important.

The first servant was forgiven a great debt, but he in turn refused to show any mercy to a fellow-servant who owed him a very small amount. When the master of both of those servants discovered what had been done, he revoked the mercy, forgiveness, and pardon that he had shown to the first servant.

There are practical ways to overcome the problem of forgiving others.

When we fail to respond with the same kind of understanding that has been given to us we are in danger of losing what we ourselves have received. No one could doubt the justice of that! It is not strange that if God has forgiven us a great debt then He would expect us to forgive others a very much smaller debt, irrespective of how serious we may consider it to be. In comparison with what God has forgiven us and the penalty that our failure rightly deserves, any forgiveness expected from us would have to be insignificant.

Delivered to the Tormentors!

The King James version of the Bible uses graphic language in describing the action of the master in dealing with the unmerciful servant. It says, *'He delivered him to the tormentors!'* The NIV says, *'In anger his master turned him over to the jailers until he should pay back all he owed'* (Matthew 18:34). The next verse makes this unequivocable statement:

> *'This is how my heavenly Father will treat each of you unless you forgive your brother from your heart.'*
> (Matthew 18:35)

That should be enough to put the fear of God into our hearts! I think it would be sobering for us to remember the words of the KJV as the phrase *'the tormentors'*, expresses what so often happens to those who refuse to forgive. The parable of the Unmerciful Servant cannot be interpreted to mean a loss of salvation to the first servant. The unjust servant was delivered to the tormentors, he was not delivered to the executioners! It is not necessary to try to explain why this translation was given in the KJV but the word 'torment' can refer to mental anguish, agony, torture, or intense bodily pain. This was the ultimate result for the unmerciful servant.

We might add that he deserved it because of his grossly selfish and uncaring attitude. But are we also guilty of such conduct?

A friend who had suffered for years because of the struggle to forgive wrote this comment to me, 'When we do not, or cannot forgive we suffer mental anguish, sometimes physical anguish, and eventual spiritual decay.'

God in Christ not only forgave but pardoned us. In comparison to this, how small are the wrongs that we have suffered.

My experience in dealing with people confirm that many are literally in torment because they will not forgive. They wonder about the origin of many of their problems, but so often it is because they will not forgive. They are still saved by the grace of God and cleansed of their sin by the blood of Christ, but they are in the hands of the tormentors because they will not forgive another, as God has forgiven them.

Let me give this illustration. I do not not think that I can remember a person more fearful, tormented, and erratic in her Christian life as this particular woman. There were occasions when she seemed to radiate Christ – days when she was exuberant and joyous – then the crash would come! She became moody, suspicious, negative, and even vindictive. She was a woman with ability and a good job, and at times her spiritual life would reach a peak of victory, but more often she would be in hopeless despair.

There were times when we wondered about her mental stability, but that was not the problem; she simply refused to forgive. The slightest incident would be interpreted as a major slight. The actions of friends would be treated as personal insults if they did not meet with her pleasure. She held grudges, dislikes, and resentment, and at times would completely ignore her friends if she was upset by some incident. I never heard her apologize; she just pretended nothing had happened after her black mood had passed.

I believe she really loved God, but she was never really willing to forgive. Her Christian life continued in this way until I finally lost contact with her when she left the church. By constant violation of the command of Jesus to forgive others, this woman was in regular mental and emotional torment.

When we forgive others we receive a positive benefit ourselves. When we hold unforgiveness toward others we become their slave as the wrong they have done to us is constantly on our mind. Forgiving another person is a liberating experience for us. But we find it hard to forgive because we don't understand God's role with regard to pardon.

Our responsibility is to be merciful toward the one who has wronged us and to be willing to dismiss from our heart the resentment we feel. We can do this by praying in a positive way for the person who has offended us. Jesus told us to love our enemies and to pray for those who persecute us (Matthew 5:44). Do not underestimate the work of the Holy Spirit as we take steps to act in obedience to God's Word. Our first steps may be reluctant and feeble but the Holy Spirit responds by helping us. The apostle Paul said we do not even know how we ought to pray, but the Holy Spirit himself intercedes for us (Romans 8:26).

> **My experience in dealing with people confirms that many are literally in torment because they will not forgive.**

What God extends to us, He expects us to extend within the scope of our authority, to others. The extent of our authority and the command to us from the Lord is to be merciful and forgiving at all times. It is not our right or prerogative to pardon. This right belongs to God!

Forgiveness – Conditional or Unconditional?

There is another major aspect. It is that God imposes conditions before forgiveness can be received. These conditions are quite clear. The first is repentance and the second is confession. God only forgives on the basis of these two conditions. If we repent and confess, then He will forgive. Our continuing fellowship with God is adversely affected by any sin, any falling short of or missing the mark that God requires for our lives. Holding bitterness or resentment is a clear violation of God's Word. If these are in our hearts toward other people, then our fellowship with God is interrupted. We are no longer walking in the light in regard to our fellowship with God.

It is interesting to note that in the Amplified Version of Matthew 6:14–15 relating to forgiving one another, the words 'giving up resentment' are used. This is the snare that believers in Christ constantly face. We are unwilling to, or do not know how to give up resentment, but we do not realize that we are placing ourselves in the hands of the 'tormentors'. Our salvation through Jesus is still a reality, but we lose the sense of the nearness of the Lord.

This leads us to a very important truth. God's heart is always open to forgive, so God requires any believer to have a similar heart attitude of willingness to forgive others irrespective of what has been done to him. There are no exceptions, we must have a heart attitude that is open to forgiveness and believe that God will impart the needed grace to do so.

It is not our right or prerogative to pardon.
This right belongs to God.

Let me confirm that God's forgiveness requires confession by the one who has sinned:

> *'If we confess our sins, he is faithful and just and will forgive us our sins and purify us from all unrighteousness.'*
> (1 John 1:9)

In other words, God will forgive us and restore us to fellowship with Him if we confess what we have done. Confession is of no value unless there is sincere sorrow for the failure, so this scripture presupposes that there has been true repentance before the confession is made. These are the unchanging grounds for forgiveness to be completed. Surely God does not require a believer to operate on a higher standard than He does? Do you think that God would expect us to have a higher level of conduct than Himself?

> *We are unwilling to give up resentment, but we do not realize that we are placing ourselves in the hands of the 'tormentors'.*

If God's forgiveness of us is not unconditional, then is our forgiveness of one another unconditional? The way we often act would make it seem that this was so! We want others to forgive and forget that we have done wrong to them by our acting as if nothing had happened. This does not work, and it does not produce genuine forgiveness as far as God is concerned.

I need to again quote the significant teaching by Jesus that we have considered in an earlier chapter, as this is vital in understanding that forgiveness between one another is not unconditional:

> *'If your brother sins against you, go and show him his fault, just between the two of you.'* (Matthew 18:15)

This command by Jesus is probably disobeyed more than any other one. We talk to other people about what we consider the wrong done to us, we gossip, we criticize, but seldom do we go and see the one with whom we have the fault. Jesus made it plain that the right course was to go direct to the person concerned and in doing this we may win our brother and the matter may be resolved. If having done this, he will not hear us, then we are to take one or two others and go to him to confirm what is being said. If then, even with the witnesses to the problem, the brother is still unwilling to listen, the issue is to go before the church.

Seldom, however, do we find that the church is willing to be involved in such personal matters, but Jesus has invested authority in the church, and the church has a vital part to play in reconciliation between conflicting members.

It is easy to reason that it is better to let an issue drop rather than beat a dead horse, but so often the unresolved problem remains like a cancer that is slowly eating away the body. Unresolved problems have a habit of exploding with a much more devastating result than the pain caused in trying to deal with them at the time they arise.

Following this teaching with the three clear steps for forgiveness, Peter came to Jesus and asked him a specific question:

> *'Lord, how many times shall I forgive my brother when he sins against me? Up to seven times?'*
> (Matthew 18:21)

I am sure that Peter thought that he was being especially gracious and spiritual as he asked that question. Up to seven times seemed a major concession because the oral law of the scribes and Pharisees provided that forgiveness be given only three times. To forgive three times was not part of the law of Moses, but it was part of the tradition that had been added to the law. It was a big step for Peter to be willing to forgive seven times! He must have been amazed by the reply given by Jesus:

> *'I tell you, not seven times, but seventy-seven times.'*
> (Matthew 18:22)

It is interesting to note that in the KJV Jesus is stated as saying to forgive seventy times seven! Whatever translation is accepted, it seems obvious that Jesus was telling

Peter that there is no limit to how often one should forgive. However, in the light of what Jesus had been saying in the previous verses, the person at fault was required to acknowledge his failure. If that was not done after the three procedures had been followed, then the penalty is quite clear:

> *'If he refuses to listen even to the church, treat him as you would a pagan or a tax collector.'*
>
> (Matthew 18:17)

God says that if we repent and confess, He will restore us to fellowship with Himself.

On many occasions I have had to deal with men and women whose attitudes and conduct have been wrong. Sometimes these people have been in positions of leadership and responsibility. Individual counselling was unsuccessful. Times of discussion with one or two others or even with an Eldership failed to gain a right response. What should have happened then? According to the teaching of Jesus, the matter should then have been taken before the whole church! Seldom does the church make provision for such an action. Perhaps we have been afraid to air dirty linen in front of the congregation and so have allowed a person to slip out of church life, often leaving the impression that the leadership and not the person was at fault!

The next news we have is that the person concerned has been given a position of responsibility in another church and his wrong action or attitude has not been dealt with. I have known men to go from a position of authority in one church to a leadership position in another church or Christian activity, leaving behind a total violation of these principles.

It is true that Jesus said we were to forgive one another, but He laid down clear rules as to what was to be done if a fault arose between brethren, and how they were to respond. And if they did not do so, then they were to be rejected from fellowship with other believers, not given a leadership role in some other sphere.

We have already seen that Jesus told Peter that forgiveness was not to be limited to a certain number of times. It would also help us to compare what Jesus said to Peter with the words of the Lord recorded in Luke's gospel:

> *'If your brother sins, rebuke him, and if he repents, forgive him. If he sins against you seven times in a day, and seven times comes back to you and says, "I repent," forgive him.'* (Luke 17:3–4)

This is a significant addition to what we have in Matthew's gospel. When people sin against us we don't just become a door mat and allow ourselves to be walked on! Jesus included the very important statement just mentioned, *'If your brother sins, rebuke him, and if he repents, forgive him.'* There are two vital actions; rebuke the one who has sinned and forgive him if he repents!

It was as a result of these words of Jesus that the disciples said to the Lord, *'increase our faith'* (Luke 17:5). The increase of faith was not for performing miracles but for the ability to repeatedly forgive. I am sure that we would feel the same

Let me summarize the situation, the brother who has sinned is first to come and repent. If there is repentance, then there are no grounds on which a Christian can hold any hurt or resentment. Repentance must bring forth the response of forgiveness. There must always be, however, even before repentance is expressed, a willingness to forgive, but the forgiveness cannot be completed unless there is repentance by the one who has caused the offence. Here we have the same consistent grounds for the completion of genuine forgiveness: repentance and confession.

There are two important categories to consider. The first one is those who are Christians, and where one has offended against another but repented. This situation often arises in church life. Someone has grieved another but comes and acknowledges the fault and repents. Forgiveness in such circumstances is to be unconditional. We have no scriptural grounds for retaining any wrong attitude or ill-will towards a person who has repented. Even if the offence is repeated, and the person once more repents, then Jesus said that he must be forgiven. There is no limit to forgiveness if repentance is shown, no matter how often one person fails another.

The increase of faith was not for performing miracles but for the ability to repeatedly forgive.

Forgiveness and Trust

Jesus did not say that we were to have the same confidence or trust in the person, but He did say that we must forgive. We have seen previously that it is possible to have fellowship restored and to forgive a person from the heart and yet still not have the same total trust or confidence in him because credibility has to be restored. This is a different matter altogether than holding unforgiveness.

The second category is when a person who has sinned against another does not repent. What happens in this case? The problem is that not many people come and say that they are sorry when an offence has been committed. Some people try to pretend that nothing has happened. They just want to forget about it. They try to renew the relationship from where the problem occurred, because they will not humble themselves and apologize.

So what do we do? This is a problem that always seems to be with us. We can only appeal to the first set of scriptures that give a general command to forgive. Our attitude must always be one of willingness to forgive, whether a person repents or not. We have the responsibility to dismiss any bitterness or resentment that we may feel irrespective of how the offender subsequently acts. If the person does not repent, then forgiveness has not been completed as far as it relates to him. He is in trouble, not with us but with God. These are not our rules they are God's!

> *We have no scriptural grounds for retaining any wrong attitude or ill-will towards a person who has repented.*

When a person does not take the initiative to put right a wrong, he remains under the 'tormentors'. The person who suffers is not the one offended against, but the one who has offended, because he remains under God's judgment. This will continue until he has humbled himself and complied with the obligation to repent and confess.

None of us is ever free of this obligation. It applies to our relationship with God and it applies to our relationship with one another. If we have sinned a specific confession is required. It is not sufficient at the end of a day to pray a general prayer asking for forgiveness. It is not as easy as that!

We need to face the reality of the principles with which we are dealing. When we know that we have deliberately disobeyed God's Word, we need to face up to it and confess it by name. God can then cleanse us and restore us to fellowship. It is the same with one another. It may first be necessary to put something right with another person or make restitution, but we must take the step to expose the problem and deal with it.

Forgiveness which must be offered at all times, is only consummated – brought to completion and perfection – when the offender repents and confesses.

Not many people come and say they are sorry when an offence has been committed.

Our danger is, that as the offended party, we can be so concerned with our brother's trespass against us that we fall into the sin of being unmerciful towards him. We fail to remember the mercy of God that has first been received by us. Jesus said that those who had been forgiven much would love much. In Luke's gospel we have these words to Simon Peter:

> *'Jesus answered him, "Simon, I have something to tell you." "Tell me teacher," he said. "Two men owed*

> *money to a certain moneylender. One owed him five*
> *hundred denarii, and the other fifty.*
> *Neither of them had the money to pay him back so he*
> *cancelled the debts of both. Now which of them will*
> *love him more?"*
> *Simon replied, "I suppose the one who had the bigger*
> *debt cancelled."*
> *"You have judged correctly," Jesus said.'*
>
> (Luke 7:40–43)

When we have been forgiven much, then we in turn should be prepared to forgive much.

Genuine Forgiveness

I want to give two examples from the Bible that illustrate the heart attitude of forgiveness. The first concerns the crucifixion of Jesus:

> *'When they came to the place called The Skull, there*
> *they crucified him, along with the criminals – one on*
> *his right, the other on his left.*
> *Jesus said, "Father, forgive them, for they do not*
> *know what they are doing." And they divided up his*
> *clothes by casting lots.'*   (Luke 23:33–34)

Jesus had been unjustly tried, tortured, and now was dying. Let me ask a question. Were all those associated with the crucifixion forgiven? When Jesus said, *'Father forgive them,'* did this mean that all the Roman soldiers, the chief priest, Pilate, and the other perpetrators of this crime were instantly forgiven? No! Jesus was demonstrating a heart attitude of willingness to forgive towards those who had falsely accused Him and nailed

Him to the Cross. In doing this Jesus kept His fellowship with God in perfect harmony. Probably those people concerned would not have been forgiven by God until each one personally repented and confessed the sin of which he was guilty.

When we have been forgiven much, then we in turn should be prepared to forgive much.

The second example concerns Stephen who was the first man to die because of his faith in Jesus Christ:

> *'While they were stoning him, Stephen prayed, "Lord Jesus, receive my spirit."*
> *Then he fell on his knees and cried out, "Lord do not hold this sin against them." When he had said this, he fell asleep.'*
> (Acts 7:59–60)

We need to ask the same question. Were all those who were stoning Stephen to death forgiven? Were they judged not guilty by God because of Stephen's prayer? No! But Stephen was demonstrating a heart attitude of willingness to forgive, even towards those who were murdering him. By this prayer Stephen's fellowship with God was unimpaired. All of those involved in killing Stephen would have needed to personally repent and confess in order to be forgiven, just as Saul, the man who later became the apostle Paul, did.

Jesus often denounced the scribes and Pharisees yet as He came near to the end of His earthly ministry He stood looking down on Jerusalem and said:

127

*'O Jerusalem, Jerusalem, you who kill the prophets
and stone those sent to you, how often I have longed
to gather your children together, as a hen gathers her
chicks under her wings, but you were not willing.'*

(Matthew 23:37)

Once again we see from Jesus a heart attitude of a
willingness to forgive in spite of the rejection He had
received, but for that forgiveness to have a practical
application in the lives of those concerned, each would
have to make a personal response.

Even Judas, the disciple who was with Jesus for more
than three years and then betrayed Him, did not receive
condemnation from the Lord. Jesus maintained an attitude of willingness to forgive at all times. An attitude
like this guarantees continuing fellowship with God.

**Stephen was demonstrating a heart attitude of
willingness to forgive, even towards those who
were murdering him.**

In summary, lack of repentance and lack of forgiveness between believers does not negate their salvation,
but it puts them in the position where God is dealing
judgmentally with them. This can result in loss of peace
and assurance in their salvation. Forgiveness does not
mean pardon. Pardon is God's responsibility. If someone has wronged us, and he or she asks to be forgiven,
then we must forgive him or her without reservation. If
there is any continuing judicial dealing of God applying
to that person, then that is God's responsibility, not
ours. Repentance and confession are always esssential

elements in true forgiveness, but God requires a forgiving heart attitude from us at all times.

We are to love one another. We have been forgiven much; we have received the mercy and pardon of God and we should be delighted to extend the same grace to others. In a hymn written by Wm R. Newell the chorus says:

> Mercy there was great and grace was free,
> Pardon there was multiplied to me,
> There my burdened soul found liberty
> At Calvary!

If we have experienced forgiveness like this, then we must be willing to forgive another person who has wronged us. Even if the other person is totally at fault, our heart attitude must still be to forgive. There are usually two sides to every dispute or difference of opinion, but even if we are 100% right and the other person is 100% wrong, we must be willing to forgive that person without any resentment remaining. Forgiveness means 'to excuse'. We must excuse or dismiss the complaint which we have.

God's actions apply in two ways. If we are in the right but are not willing to forgive, we come under God's discipline. If we are in the wrong but will not repent and confess, we also come under God's discipline. We can have the situation where both the one who is right and the one who is wrong are under God's judgment because they will not have the right attitude or will not take the right action.

In other words, both the unforgiving and the unrepentant suffer the consequences of their own disobedience to the principles of God's Word.

'Brothers, if someone is caught in a sin, you who are spiritual should restore him gently. But watch yourself, or you also may be tempted.

Carry each other's burdens, and in this way you will fulfil the law of Christ.

If anyone thinks he is something when he is nothing, He deceives himself.

Each one should test his own actions. Then he can take pride in himself, without comparing himself to someone else, for each one should carry his own load.

Anyone who receives instruction in the word must share all good things with his instructor.

Do not be deceived: God cannot be mocked. A man reaps what he sows.

The one who sows to please his sinful nature, from that nature will reap destruction; the one who sows to please the Spirit, from the Spirit will reap eternal life.

Let us not become weary in doing good, for at the proper time we will reap a harvest if we do not give up.' (Galatians 6:1–9)

Chapter 5

Sowing and Reaping

Our studies so far have made clear from scripture that although mercy and forgiveness and some degree of pardon have been extended by God that it is possible to continue to suffer the consequences of sin and failure. This was illustrated in a previous chapter from the life of King David who, although sincerely and genuinely repenting of the sin he had committed, and who was forgiven and restored to fellowship with God, remained under a temporal judgment of God. David wrote after he had repented, of the blessing for the man whose transgressions were forgiven and whose sin the Lord did not count against him (Psalm 32:1–2), yet God had declared that the *'sword would never depart from his house'* (2 Samuel 12:10). It is important as we continue to study the subject of biblical forgiveness that we remember this principle.

A Creative Principle

It is necessary to elaborate on this aspect. God has built into life a creative principle that is known as 'sowing and reaping'. In a natural way, it applies to crops and the plants that we grow. We must first sow before we can reap. We will never obtain a harvest of wheat or any other grain or plant if we do not first sow the seed. We will not get the vegetables we enjoy and need for good health if the seeds are not planted. This is true in a natural way and it is also true spiritually with regard to our daily actions.

Reaping what we have sown can continue, even after forgiveness has been received from God, or even when it has been received from man. I want to refer to some important scriptures:

> *'As I have observed, those who plough evil and those who sow trouble reap it.'* (Job 4:8)

> *'The wicked man earns deceptive wages, but he who sows righteousness reaps a sure reward.'* (Proverbs 11:18)

> *'He who sows wickedness reaps trouble, and the rod of his fury will be destroyed.'* (Proverbs 22:8)

All of these scriptures are important in recognizing that we will reap whatever we sow. In the prophecy of Hosea we read:

> *'They sow the wind and reap the whirlwind. The stalk has no head; it will produce no flour. Were it to yield grain, foreigners would swallow it up.'* (Hosea 8:7)

In the same book of the Bible we find this statement:

> *'Sow for yourselves righteousness, reap the fruit of unfailing love, and break up your unploughed ground;*

for it is time to seek the Lord, until he comes and showers righteousness on you.
But you have planted wickedness, you have reaped evil, you have eaten the fruit of deception. Because you have depended on your own strength and on your many warriors.'
(Hosea 10:12–13)

Reaping what we have sown can continue, even after forgiveness has been received from God, or even when it has been received from man.

All of these scriptures tell us that whatever we are ploughing and sowing will come back to us. If it is evil and iniquity, or selfishness and pride, the same will return to us. There is no escape from the divine principle of reaping what we sow, whether it be in a natural or spiritual sense!

In Paul's letter to the Galatians this principle is again confirmed. The relevant passage begins with the words, *'Do not be deceived'* (Galatians 6:7). There are many people today who are deceived, and they are willing to be deceived, because they will not accept this clear truth from God's Word. Sometimes it seems that God is slow in acting on what He has said. This is because of His mercy and His willingness to allow time for repentance, but inevitably God will act on what He has said. The verse says:

'Do not be deceived; God cannot be mocked. A man reaps what he sows.
The one who sows to please his sinful nature, from that nature will reap destruction; the one who sows to

> *please the Spirit, from the Spirit, will reap eternal life.'*
> (Galatians 6:7–8)

My father is now deceased, but was eighty-seven years of age when he died. As a young married man, in his mid-thirties, he had a personal experience of receiving Christ as his Saviour and Lord, but prior to this he had no particular involvement with the church, nor did he have extensive spiritual knowledge. He worked in a hard environment where drinking and swearing were a normal part of life.

I am the youngest member of a large family and my oldest sister, as a small girl walked from our home to a nearby Baptist church one Sunday morning and sat on the steps and listened to the congregation singing. She came home and said to my father, 'Daddy, will you take me to church?' To humour the little girl he said, 'Yes, dear, I'll do it next week.' It was just an easy reply for him and not for one moment did he think that my sister would remember the promise, but she did! When the Sunday came, she reminded him, and he reluctantly honoured the promise and took my sister to the church.

He was deeply moved by the service and returned to the church that evening with my mother, and at the close of the meeting committed his life to Christ. He remembered only one part of the sermon, the text from which the minister preached, *'God is not mocked, for whatsoever a man soweth that shall he also reap.'* My father received Jesus Christ into his life because of the conviction that came through that verse of scripture. He realized that he was sowing a life of self-pleasing and sin, and was suddenly faced with the fact that he would ultimately reap the same result if his life did not change. His spiritual awakening and obedience to the conviction of the Holy Spirit that night changed the destiny of our family and ultimately all the family members came to know the Lord in a personal way.

A man reaps what he sows.

Negative and Positive

In all the scriptures that have been quoted, there is a negative and positive aspect. This is evident throughout the Word of God. In the verses just quoted, the negative results are – plough evil and reap evil. Sow trouble and reap trouble. Sow to the wind and reap the whirlwind. Plant wickedness and reap evil. All of these are negative results that arise out of our own actions.

I want to include another personal experience concerning a man whom I met on several occasions. He was part of another church congregation, but from time-to-time I visited that church and also had contact with other members of his family. He was difficult and rigid and seldom smiled although if something pleased him, he could be warm and complimentary. It wasn't a comforting sight to see him sitting in the congregation as he listened with a fixed look on his face. Was he approving or disapproving? He was even willing to publicly question a novice preacher in the midst of a sermon if he disagreed with some statement.

There were times when he could be generous, but he was feared more than he was liked. How much happier life could have been for him, but his negative and often critical attitude caused him to see the worst rather than the best in most aspects of life.

A church function was planned and excitement and generosity were the order of the day. This man grew in his garden a particular vegetable that was required and a request was made: could he supply the quantity needed? The need was not large, and his supply was quite abundant, but when the box of produce was handed over the demand was made, 'That will be $10!'

He died a rather lonely man, devoid of much friendship that could have been his. The word of God was a subject of deep interest to him, but what is the value of knowledge if we cannot implement it? One can know the words but not know what they mean! The small gift of vegetables would have been a minor contribution to that which others of far less means gladly made, but the incident marked him as a man lacking in generosity.

Extra money may have been his, but he lost love, friendship, and respect as a result of his miserly spirit. Do we reap what we sow? Of this fact, I have no doubt!

There is, however, the positive result as well. The Bible always has a positive provision that releases a person from a negative penalty into a positive benefit, so we also have these promises:

'The wicked man earns deceptive wages, but he who sows righteousness reaps a sure reward.'
(Proverbs 11:18)

'Sow for yourselves righteousness, reap the fruit of unfailing love.' (Hosea 10:12)

'The one who sows to please his sinful nature, from that nature will reap destruction; the one who sows to please the Spirit will reap eternal life.'
(Galatians 6:8)

These are the choices that are laid before us. Whatever we do in life, from all our attitudes and actions, will come forth a definite result either for good or ill. There is no escaping from this. From everything we sow we will reap, so we have the choice of whether we want beneficial or harmful consequences as we proceed through life.

The Word of the Lord always has a positive provision that releases one from a negative penalty into a positive benefit.

Here is an opposite example from the stingy man just mentioned. It would be hard to imagine a more generous person than a woman I knew. Nothing was a trouble, and no sacrifice was too great. In fact, I am sure she never thought of giving as a sacrifice, but as a privilege. If someone was sick; dishes of food would be prepared without any asking. A busy mother trying to cope with the washing, ironing, and cooking for a family of six lively, hungry children, would suddenly hear a knock at the door and there she would be, ready to do a stint of two hours at the hot ironing board.

Her company was a joy! Her very presence radiated warmth and restored strength to those she helped. She never did manage to accumulate much money in the bank, but if wealth was measured in appreciation, love and admiration, she was a millionaire!

This principle of sowing and reaping continues throughout scripture, both in the Old Testament and in the New Testament. The words 'sowing and reaping' may not always be used, but the outcome is the same.

Think for a moment of the Babylonian king,
Nebuchadnezzar. The Bible tells how this man was filled
with pride and self adulation because of his conquests
and power. He considered himself above God. There is
an incident recorded in the Book of Daniel where,
because of Nebuchadnezzar's pride, the judgment of
God came upon him. These words are recorded:

> *'Immediately what had been said about Nebuchad-*
> *nezzar was fulfilled. He was driven away from people*
> *and ate grass like cattle. His body was drenched with*
> *the dew of heaven until his hair grew like the feathers*
> *of an eagle and his nails like the claws of a bird.'*
>
> (Daniel 4:33)

This powerful king who had enslaved so many peoples
and nations suddenly began to reap God's judgment and
punishment because of the pride that was in his heart.
God is not mocked, and any person will ultimately and
certainly reap what he has sown.

In the next chapter of the Book of Daniel, we read of
Belshazzar. The opening verses of chapter 5 say:

> *'King Belshazzar gave a great banquet for a thousand*
> *of his nobles and drank wine with them.*
> *While Belshazzar was drinking his wine, he gave*
> *orders to bring in the gold and silver goblets that*
> *Nebuchadnezzar his father had taken from the temple*
> *in Jerusalem, so that the king and his nobles, his wives*
> *and his concubines might drink from them.*
> *So they brought in the gold goblets that had been*
> *taken from the temple of God in Jerusalem, and the*
> *king and his nobles, his wives and his concubines*
> *drank from them.*

> *As they drank the wine, they praised the gods of gold*
> *and silver, of bronze, iron, wood and stone.'*
>
> (Daniel 5:1–4)

This man was sowing! He was sowing the seeds of blasphemy and disregard for the sacred vessels from the temple of the Lord. As we read through the chapter, we find the judgment of God being pronounced on him, and in the final part of the chapter we read:

> *'That very night Belshazzar, king of the Babylonians,*
> *was slain, and Darius the Mede took over the king-*
> *dom...'*
>
> (Daniel 5:30–31)

Belshazzar thought that he could blaspheme God, but he reaped judgment.

In the New Testament we read of King Herod. This man's evil actions are recorded in many places throughout the scripture. Brutality and murder were but some of the crimes of which he was guilty. The principle of sowing and reaping as it applied to Herod's life is recorded in Acts 12:

> *'On the appointed day Herod, wearing his royal*
> *robes, sat on his throne and delivered a public address*
> *to the people.*
> *They shouted, "This is the voice of a god, not a man."*
> *Immediately, because Herod did not give praise to*
> *God, an angel of the Lord struck him down, and he*
> *was eaten by worms and died.'* (Acts 12:21–23)

This was another operation of the unchanging truth of sowing and reaping. Herod reaped from what he had sown.

It would be possible to give many other instances from the Bible where individuals or nations received a direct penalty as a result of their actions. One example would be the children of Israel who were taken into slavery because of disobedience. So often we read of individuals, nations, kings or servants, who were afflicted, diseased, or suffered other distressing circumstances as a direct result of their own evil actions.

Sowing and the Increase

It is important that we remember that reaping is normally in greater measure than that which is sown. The Bible speaks of a seed which brings forth thirty or sixty or a hundredfold. Seldom do we plant one seed or one flower and get only one back again. There is a multiplication which takes place because of the sowing. An action for good or ill, which may seem to be minor, may have far-reaching and devastating results in a person's life. We may say, 'That wasn't anything very serious, God wouldn't be concerned about that.' One small seed, however, can produce a large result.

It was many years ago that the following events took place, but I vividly remember them. I approached the house with a feeling of trepidation, yet excitement because I was a young and inexperienced pastor. The name of the occupant of the house had been sent to me by the counselling committee of the Billy Graham crusade, my very first contact! What kind of a response would I get? My knock on the door was a little uncertain, but was loud enough to bring a response, and the door opened. He stood framed in the doorway, a big man with a hard face and I felt like a David confronting his Goliath!

My words of introduction tumbled out and I received a warm welcome, and was soon seated with him in the living room. It was the beginning of a mixture of experiences. In the years that lay ahead, I was to receive from this man warm friendship, support, unreliability, dishonesty, repentance, egotistical behaviour, drunkenness, spiritual affirmations of desire to live a consistent Christian life, and then watch him face bankruptcy and the ultimate breakdown of his marriage. A man with so much potential who ultimately reaped from the seeds of selfishness and sin that he continued to sow.

There is a multiplication which takes place through sowing.

He wanted God in his life, but he also wanted his own way. The war years had made him tough and somewhat ruthless. Commando training had built a violence that would often rise up within him, but he was likeable and easy to forgive.

My new church needed all the manpower possible, and he began to help with the youth work, but alcohol was an occasional problem although he would deny it. We helped him start in business, but he misused opportunities and spent money needed to pay sub-contractors for his own pleasure and for keeping up a pretence that he was a wealthy businessman.

I could not count the hours that others and I spent with him. We prayed, pleaded, and even wept, but every act of repentance by him was followed by an act of selfishness or foolishness. The seed was small when it was first sown, but it brought forth a harvest of despair and destruction. I would like to write of a happy ending but it didn't happen. After I left the area and then moved to another country I heard of his bankruptcy, adultery and divorce.

The years passed without hearing anything about him, then not long ago he attended a meeting which I was conducting in the city where he was living. He had seen my name advertised and had come to the meeting. He was in the last stages of terminal cancer, but I had the opportunity to pray with him and then write to him before he died. I believe that he had made his peace with God, but I still mourn when I think of the wasted possibilities of his life.

I have already quoted the scripture, *'Sow the wind and reap the whirlwind'* (Hosea 8:7). Most days, the wind is blowing. Even if the wind becomes strong, it is normally not a problem. The expression *'sow to the wind'* is illustrating a natural climatic operation of the wind. If, however, a whirlwind occurs, that is entirely different.

If you have experienced a whirlwind, or a tornado, or cyclone, you will know that it is very different from the wind that blows day-by-day. We experience cyclones in the part of the world where I live, and I have experienced many severe storms and cyclones over the years and have seen their devastating effect. In the secular occupation which I was engaged in for many years as an independent Loss Adjuster, both in New Zealand and Australia, I was involved in the assessment of damage caused by most of the storms that occurred in those years. I have seen the effects of a whirlwind! I have seen roofs ripped from houses and strongly constructed buildings destroyed like matchwood. I have seen ruin left in the path of cyclones. Yet day after day, the wind had blown over those houses and buildings and no damage occurred, but suddenly, because of the whirlwind, there was destruction.

Sow the wind and reap the whirlwind.

On the 10th April 1968 a devastating storm struck the city of Wellington in New Zealand and I was an eye witness to perhaps the worst storm ever to strike that part of the world.

The southerly wind lashed at the houses and commercial buildings near to the coast and on the exposed hillsides. Buildings designed to resist the most severe winds could not withstand the violence of the storm and were wrecked. The large inter-island motor vessel *Wahine* was caught by the violence of the storm as the ship attempted to enter the Wellington Harbour, and was carried on to a reef and wrecked. Miraculously, the majority of passengers and crew were saved although over fifty people were drowned.

Who could imagine a scene like this? For months my office was inundated with the assessment of thousands of claims for damage. We employed extra men and women to help us cope with the sheer volume of work as a result of the devastation. For over four months I worked from 7 a.m. to 10 p.m. every day, and most weeks this included Sunday.

I know what a storm can do! It can change a scene of beauty and tranquility to one of horror and destruction. I have a deep appreciation of what the Bible means when it declares, *'Sow the wind and reap the whirlwind!'*

When the scripture says that we are no longer dealing with the wind, but with a whirlwind, it graphically illustrates the increase that can come from what we sow by

143

our actions. The seed that is planted seems small but the results which suddenly confront us are devastating. We need to think seriously about this analogy used in God's Word.

Let me now deal with the positive benefits of sowing and reaping. We can sow that which God approves and blesses and in turn reap thirty, sixty, and a hundred times of the blessings of God. Jesus said:

> *' "Well done, my good servant!" his master replied. "Because you have been trustworthy in a very small matter, take charge of ten cities." '*   (Luke 19:17)

In this parable a small amount of faithfulness reaped a large reward. The good that we sow is magnified as is the evil that we sow. Whatever we sow will be greater in the reaping than in the sowing. How foolish then, that we should sow to the negative when we have been told clearly that we will reap a far greater negative result when we can, instead, sow to the positive and receive abundant blessings and provision.

The seed that is planted seems small but the results which suddenly confront us are devastating.

We need to live to please God and not just to please ourselves. We often look at events from a short term point of view, but God is looking at them in the long-term. When we plant seeds in a garden, we do not expect to see the harvest spring up immediately. There is a time lapse. We may sow disobedience and evil and for a time see nothing adverse, but the principle is in operation and an inevitable result will follow.

There is an incident in the life of Jesus when a Roman centurion appealed to Jesus to heal a servant who was sick. When Jesus offered to go to the centurion's house the man replied:

> *'Lord, I do not deserve to have you come under my roof. But just say the word, and my servant will be healed.'*
> (Matthew 8:8)

Jesus was amazed at the faith shown by the centurion and said:

> *'I tell you the truth, I have not found anyone in Israel with such great faith.'*
> (Matthew 8:10)

As a result of the faith in Jesus shown by the centurion, his servant was healed. The centurion, by planting a seed of faith, received a harvest of God's healing in the life of his servant.

God wants to increase the good that He desires for our lives. God is merciful and will always inflict less upon us than the legal punishment that we deserve, so if sin returns an increase, it should make us understand how serious sin is to God. A holy God and sin of any kind is incompatible!

The good that we sow is magnified, as is the evil that we sow. Whatever we sow will be greater in the reaping than in the sowing.

Sowing by the Unbeliever

The principle of sowing and reaping as it applies to people in three different categories are as follows:
• The unbeliever.
• The person who is converted to Christ.
• The Christian in his spiritual life.

The question we need to answer is this: what does forgiveness provide for the person in these three different categories, and how does the principle of sowing and reaping apply to him?

The Unbeliever

The Bible says, *'The wages of sin is death'* (Romans 6:23). It also says, *'The soul who sins is the one who will die'* (Ezekiel 18:20). The person who does not accept by faith the salvation that is offered through Jesus Christ, is under sentence of eternal separation from God, because the Bible also says, *'All have sinned'* (Romans 3:23). None of us is righteous! The best of our actions fail to come up to the standard required by a holy God.

The unbeliever may continue to enjoy certain temporal benefits and blessings that come from the general mercy of God. We have seen before how God gives the benefits of the different seasons to both the just and the unjust alike. God is not restricted to applying the law of sowing and reaping in this life alone. God's ways are eternal, so the truth of sowing and reaping will continue to apply. The unbeliever goes on receiving a measure of the mercy and the goodness of God and may prosper in a material way. Some unbelievers may continue to prosper all their lives, even though they have acted unjustly.

We need to realize that the eternal consequences of

reaping what we have sown are far more drastic and important than the temporal aspect. I would rather reap the blessings of God eternally than now, if I had to make a choice. This life is described in the scripture as *'a mist that appears for a little while and then vanishes'* (James 4:14). God has promised us only a limited life span at the best, but eternity is unending. This life is God's training ground for what lies ahead of us in eternity.

We find, however, that some people reap very quickly the results of their way of life, and such cases are not isolated. There are people in the world who have reaped quickly from what they have sown. We could think of some wealthy people whose ways of business have been unscrupulous and dishonest. They have built financial empires, but only to see what they have built collapse around them. There are many such cases at the present time and some of those involved have ended in bankruptcy and even prison.

We could think of the famous who have reached a place of prominence through deceit or selfishness, and then suddenly had their actions exposed and their reputations ruined.

The eternal consequences of reaping what we have sown are far more drastic and important than the temporal aspect.

We do not have to go back far in contemporary history to recall leaders of nations who were suddenly disgraced because they were sowing seeds of dishonesty, and suddenly these sprang up into sight and were exposed. The same is true of some religious and church leaders. They reaped what they had sown!

We often read of men and women in the entertainment industry who died, some at a young age, because of what they had sown in their own lives. They reaped quickly! They had sown to the wind and truly reaped a whirlwind. Often, it had been a whirlwind of disease or mental disorder. Some have sown seeds of corruption by drug abuse and every kind of excess and perversion, and suddenly the whirlwind came.

God allows some to reap quickly from their sin and others to appear to continue to prosper, but the opening verses of Psalm 37 are appropriate for us to remember:

'Do not fret because of evil men or be envious of those who do wrong; for like the grass they will soon wither, like green plants they will soon die away.
Trust in the Lord and do good; dwell in the land and enjoy safe pasture.'　　　　　　　　　　(Psalm 37:1–3)

The psalm continues with these words:

'For evil men will be cut off, but those who hope in the Lord will inherit the land.
A little while, and the wicked will be no more; though you look for them they will not be found.'
　　　　　　　　　　　　　　　　　　(Psalm 37:9–10)

One thing is sure: the unbeliever will ultimately reap from his sin. He will reap from it eternal judgment and separation from God, apart from any temporal judgment that his sin may invoke.

What Happens at Conversion?

The Person Who is Converted to Christ

We come now to the second category. How does the law of sowing and reaping apply in this person's life? The Bible declares that the blood of Jesus Christ, God's Son, cleanses us from all sin. Paul, writing to the Corinthian church said:

> *'Therefore, if anyone is in Christ, he is a new creation; the old has gone, the new has come!'*
>
> (2 Corinthians 5:17)

The Living Bible paraphrase of this verse says:

> *'When someone becomes a Christian, he becomes a brand new person inside. He is not the same any more. A new life has begun.'*

This is a clear statement, but often it does not seem to happen! People receive Christ and it does not seem that the old things pass away. There are hurts, wounds, and disappointments that remain, allowing negative attitudes to dominate them.

One thing is sure – the unbeliever will ultimately reap from his sin.

I want to give the illustration of a young man I knew. He had a great start to his Christian life. His brother was a fine Christian young man and we had prayed for the salvation of his brother for some time before he finally came to church. The two brothers came to our home for a snack at the close of that Sunday night service, and we talked about the need to receive Christ in a personal way.

I explained the way of salvation and asked if he would like to receive Christ into his life. He replied in the affirmative and I began to lead him in a prayer of repentance and acceptance of Jesus. No words came from his mouth! I repeated the simple prayer, but still no words came. As we looked at him his mouth seemed to be locked, and try as he would, no words would come!

We discerned that he was bound by some demonic spirit, and we began to speak against it in the Name of Jesus. Suddenly he was free! The prayer flowed from his lips and the joyous change in his whole appearance was amazing. Later that night he and his brother were physically attacked by demonic forces to the extent that the older brother fell to the floor, apparently unconscious. Again, we claimed the authority in the Name of Jesus and saw complete deliverance.

Let me assure you that this is not an illustration of some extreme attitude to deliverance. Never before or since have I had a similar experience. God's power was marvellously provided for the release of this young man and for the protection of his older brother.

We saw the younger brother press on in the Christian life for some months, but then he began to doubt and allowed old negative fears and attitudes that had previously plagued his life to return. His Christian life became inconsistent. A moodiness that had been a problem and which had vanished with his conversion returned, and his spiritual life became weak and indifferent. I am glad to say that in later years he recaptured the blessing and peace of God and today he is involved with a lively effective church, but he spent some years in struggling to overcome his weaknesses.

Should our spiritual experience be like this, or do we often fail to appropriate all that is available through our faith in Christ? There can be a big gap in the lives of people between what they have 'possessionally', that is, what they actually experience in their lives and what they have 'positionally', that is, the fullness of what God has provided in Jesus Christ. I am sure that many of the problems that Christians face today are because they have not discovered how to receive what Jesus has actually provided for them. It is our appropriation that is defective and not the provisions of the Word of God or the power of the Holy Spirit.

Man is a tripartite being comprising spirit, soul, and body. There is a total provision in all of these areas through the sacrifice of Christ on the Cross. There is healing for our spirit from the effect of sin and also from a wounded spirit. The spirit is the inner spiritual part of a person, the part that has an affinity with God. There is healing for the soul. The soul is the area of the natural man, involving mind, emotions and will. Healing was provided for these faculties when Jesus took our griefs and sorrows upon Himself. The death of Jesus also provided access to physical healing for our bodies. The death of Jesus Christ on the Cross was a complete defeat of Satan and a complete victory for Jesus. By His death and then His resurrection, provision was made for all our needs.

We realize, however, that God is working a sovereign plan and we cannot demand that all our needs be immediately met because His timing is not our timing. We are challenged by the Word of God to be 'overcomers', to come through every test and trial as winners and not losers, to stand firm and trust God whatever may be happening. We are required to live our lives in hope, with an eager and confident expectation of good regardless of our circumstances, and we need to learn how to appropriate all that Christ has provided for us, rather than allow our past problems to dominate us.

> *It is our appropriation that is defective and not the provisions of the Word of God.*

When a person accepts Christ as Saviour the principle of sowing and reaping from an eternal perspective is lifted. God no longer inflicts the penalties which would otherwise be applicable because of sins committed by the person prior to his salvation. The slate is wiped clean from the penalty and guilt of all past sin. What a fantastic provision that is! Salvation does not, however, save a person from the temporal consequences of a crime of which he or she may be guilty. God has cleared the record and there will be no eternal penalty, but the person may still be accountable to the civil authorities.

It is a tragedy, however, that so many Christians through unwillingness to accept that God has really forgiven them, and through unbelief, fear, and doubt, allow old attitudes to continue and so bring about a negative reaping in their lives. In doing this, the person reduces in his own life some of the wonderful provisions of the Cross. The new convert, and also the experienced Christian, must constantly allow his mind to be renewed, his emotions to be purified and his will to be set free so as to accept the forgiveness that God has given, and to harmonize with God's will for his life. Unfortunately, we find in experience, that born again Christians are still reaping in a spiritual sense from events that happened before they were saved. This should not be!

When one receives Christ *'the old is gone, the new has come!'* (2 Corinthians 5:17). This is the promise, but we are then faced with the challenge of making this real in our daily experience.

Many Christians through unbelief and fear, allow old attitudes to continue, and so bring about a negative reaping in their lives.

Our New Life in Christ

The Christian in His Siritual Life

This is the third category.

The 'new birth' provides a fresh start from God's point of view, but from then on we again become accountable for our actions. The law of sowing and reaping once more becomes part of our life as it was before conversion. Mercy and forgiveness are always available but consequences are a reality to be faced. In John's first letter we read:

'This is the message we have heard from him and declare to you: God is light; in him there is no darkness at all.
If we claim to have fellowship with him yet walk in the darkness, we lie and do not live by the truth.
But if we walk in the light, as he is in the light, we have fellowship with one another, and the blood of Jesus, his Son, purifies us from all sin.'

(1 John 1:5–7)

This is the promise of God. He cleanses us and restores us to fellowship with him, but the promise is for forgiveness and fellowship, not pardon. There are failures that have to be dealt with. We may have thought that all was well. One might say to himself:

'Yes, I did treat that person badly, but it happened a long time ago and perhaps it is now forgotten.'

'I would be too embarrassed to go back now and apologize.'

'Yes I did let them down. I told lies about them.'

Until wrongs are put right, we can go on suffering the consequences of what we have sown!

We cannot put back the clock to the day when we were first saved, when, if only we had understood these principles, how different our Christian life might have been. We can, however, avail ourselves now of God's grace and humble ourselves both before God, and our brother if necessary, in order to break the cycle of reaping what we have sown.

It is vital to emphasize a truth that has previously been mentioned. We can be without fault in a dispute, but because we are unforgiving, God's judgment still rests upon us because we will reap the penalty of unforgiveness. The guilty party also is not excused as, even if he is forgiven, God's dealings may continue until the right responses are made.

We do not need to be bound by the failures of the past. We can start reaping the fruit of righteousness and not the fruit of unrighteousness. We do not need to reap a whirlwind but we can reap the blessings and rewards of God. As we accept the provisions of the Cross, fulfil God's conditions and walk in obedience to Him, this can be our experience.

A young married man in a leadership position in a church gave me this testimony:

> I had the privilege of a fine, stable home life and at the age of thirteen years was considered a decent kid. I had attended a denominational church but knew nothing about a personal experience of knowing Jesus Christ as Saviour and Lord.
>
> At this age I began to desire acceptance from others of my own age group, many of whom were involved in immorality and drinking. This desire increased as I progressed through high school, and to gain the esteem of the other boys I began to create a web of lies about myself and my activities. These lies increased to such an extent that by my early twenties the real me was a stranger to myself!
>
> My teen years gave me the opportunity to develop a life style in which I doubted the existence of God, and considered Christianity a middle class social club.
>
> By the time I reached twenty-one years, I was a heavy drinker and was involved in every kind of conduct contrary to my early upbringing. My life was a mess of falsehood as I tried to keep up with the image I had created for myself, but deep within there was insecurity, depression, and self-pity. I wore a knife strapped to my leg, and on occasions carried a shotgun in the back of my car in order to feed my ego as a 'tough man'!
>
> In this situation a despair began to grip my fiancée and me and I began to search for some spiritual answer. We tried spiritualism, eastern mysticism, and philosophy, but these merely made us critical of existing religions and social patterns.

My fiancée and I married and decided to spend some time fruit picking. The orchard owners were evangelical Christians and we were deeply challenged by the message of the Gospel but seemed unable to reach a place of total acceptance of Christ's way.

We moved from New Zealand to Sydney, Australia, and again became associated with Christians and were increasingly convicted of the degree of falsehood that was in both of our lives. The Holy Spirit was dealing with us, and old fears and prejudices were beginning to crumble. One Saturday night we attended a film service in a local Pentecostal Church. Both my wife and I responded to the invitation to receive Christ as Saviour, and one week later were baptized in water. Within a short time we were both baptized with the Holy Spirit.

What a change! All those years of pretending to be something that I wasn't and trying to find a satisfaction that remained beyond my grasp. Now it was over! God had many things to do in my life. He dealt with pride, unwillingness to be submissive, and self effort, but we had found something real and meaningful in our lives.

I praise God for His grace and power. When I fully realized that I was in a race of life and God's way was the only way and there was no way back, I almost panicked, wondering if I could make it! Then I realized that the strength and ability were His, not mine. My wife and I now desire to be totally committed to the Lord Jesus Christ and to live God's way by the power of the Holy Spirit. Truly, old things are passed away.

We do not need to be bound by the things of the past. We can start reaping the fruit of righteousness and not the fruit of unrighteousness.

'And we know that in all things God works for the good of those who love him, who have been called according to his purpose.

For those God foreknew he also predestined to be conformed to the likeness of his Son, that he might be the firstborn among many brothers.

And those he predestined, he also called; those he called, he also justified; those he justified, he also glorified.

What, then, shall we say in response to this? If God is for us, who can be against us? He who did not spare his own Son, but gave him up for us all – how will he not also, along with him, graciously give us all things?

Who will bring any charge against those whom God has chosen? It is God who justifies.

Who is he that condemns? Christ Jesus, who died – more than that, who was raised to life – is at the right hand of God and is also interceding for us.

Who shall separate us from the love of Christ? Shall trouble or hardship or persecution or famine or nakedness or danger or sword?

As it is written: "For your sake we face death all day long; we are considered as sheep to be slaughtered."

No, in all these things we are more than conquerors through him who loved us.

For I am convinced that neither death nor life, neither angels nor demons, neither the present nor the future, nor any powers, neither height nor depth, nor anything else in all creation, will be able to separate us from the love of God that is in Christ Jesus our Lord.'   (Romans 8:28–39)

Chapter 6

What is Happening?

An unusual title has been chosen for this chapter because of what people have said to me. On many occasions I have talked with men and women who were experiencing problems and difficulties and they have said, 'What is happening? I do not understand what is taking place in my life!'

I want to refer to three different passages of scripture, and they need to be read so that the comparison can be clearly seen. The first, found in Romans 8:28–39, has been set out on the feature page of this chapter.

The second scripture is found in The Book of Judges:

> 'The angel of the Lord went up from Gilgal to Bokim and said, "I brought you up out of Egypt and led you into the land that I swore to give to your forefathers. I said, 'I will never break my covenant with you, and you shall not make a covenant with the people of this land, but you shall break down their altars.' Yet you have disobeyed me. Why have you done this?
> Now therefore I tell you that I will not drive them out before you; they will be thorns in your sides and their gods will be a snare to you." '   (Judges 2:1–3)

The third scripture is found in the letter to the Hebrew church:

> *'And you have forgotten that word of encouragement that addresses you as sons:*
> *"My son, do not make light of the Lord's discipline, and do not lose heart when he rebukes you, because the Lord disciplines those he loves, and he punishes everyone he accepts as a son."*
> *Endure hardship as discipline; God is treating you as sons. For what son is not disciplined by his father?*
> *If you are not disciplined (and everyone undergoes discipline), then you are illegitimate children and not true sons.*
> *Moreover, we have all had human fathers who disciplined us and we respected them for it. How much more should we submit to the Father of our spirits and live!*
> *Our fathers disciplined us for a little while as they thought best; but God disciplines us for our good, that we may share in his holiness.'*   (Hebrews 12:5–10)

Three Alternatives

We have quoted these scriptures in full for an important reason. In these passages we have three vastly contrasting aspects. The verses in Romans 8:28–39 speak of the promises and provisions of God so that in spite of every kind of difficulty and testing we can be confident that God is still with us, and we can live triumphantly. Promises of strengthening and help are given so that those who love God and are called by Him will stand firm and not be shaken in their faith and hope regardless of their circumstances.

The second scripture (Judges 2:1–3) refers to a people chosen by God who, under His direction, went in to possess the land of Canaan that had been promised to them. The enemy was confronted and the land conquered often in miraculous ways. But later the people of Israel became disobedient to God, and because of their disobedience, suffered opposition and attack from the original occupants of the land. God declared that the Canaanites would now become 'thorns in the sides of the Israelites and the gods of the land of Canaan would become a snare to them' (Judges 2:3). The Israelites were a privileged people and God had been with them, but now they were rebuked and judged.

The third scripture (Hebrews 12:5–10) tells of a loving heavenly Father disciplining His children out of concern and care because He loves them and wants to see them grow and develop into the likeness of Christ.

People have spoken to me of problems and difficulties in home life, personal relationships, or in their work, and although they had taken apparent steps of trust in God their efforts had ended in a blind alley! In confusion and not knowing where they were going in life, they had come for counsel, pouring out a story of despair and had said, 'What is happening?'

Cause and Effect

From what has been said in the last chapter dealing with reaping and sowing there are some aspects that must now be clarified. The question that confronts us is what are the reasons for the challenges, problems, and difficulties that occur in our daily lives? They can be summarized under three headings:

1. Have we failed to appropriate the total provisions of the Cross?

We have already dealt with the total redemptive work of the Cross and have seen how Jesus gave Himself as a sacrifice in body, soul, and spirit. He made it possible for our spirit to be born anew and indwelt by the Spirit of God so that we might become part of a new creation. He poured out his soul to death and bore our griefs and sorrows and dealt with every influence that touches our mind, emotions, and will.

Some Bible teachers have emphasized the subject of inner healing and healing of memories, but Jesus made provision for this on the Cross when He suffered in the realm of the soul. There may be lingering results from some of our past experiences, but we should not need to receive protracted ministry or prayer for such problems.

The prophet Isaiah declared, *'By his wounds we are healed'* (Isaiah 53:5). A provision has been made for physical healing through the suffering and sacrifice of Christ on Calvary.

If we have unexplainable problems, the first question we must ask ourselves is are we appropriating the full benefits of what Christ has already done for us?

2. Are we reaping what we have sown?

Every action has a result! There is nothing that we do that is isolated, but as we have dealt with this subject in detail it is not necessary to elaborate. Let us, however, note carefully that every action we take will have a result for good or ill, so when we are faced with confusion or difficulty, we need to make an honest evaluation as to whether we are reaping a negative result from what we have sown.

3. Is God, through these difficult circumstances, disciplining us and pruning our lives because of His love and care?

The scripture says:

> '...*because the Lord disciplines those he loves, and he punishes everyone he accepts as a son.*'
>
> (Hebrews 12:6)

Jesus gave teaching that is similar to this:

> '*I am the true vine and my Father is the gardener. He cuts off every branch in me that bears no fruit, while every branch that does bear fruit he prunes so that it will be even more fruitful.*'   (John 15:1–2)

Every action we take will have a result for good or ill.

In times of difficulty, uncertainty, or testing we are faced with these three alternatives. Which of these three reasons apply? We must know so that we can find peace or, if there is a wrong to be put right, take action to bring about a solution.

The problem we all have is to be genuinely objective when we try to evaluate what is happening to us. We all see things from our own point of view. Most Christians are sincere in their desire to serve God, but we all look at events from our own perspective. It is very natural to say, 'Be reasonable, do it my way!' We are usually convinced that our way is right, so it is hard to look at the problem from all angles and particularly to recognize that we all have some blind spots. We do not see it because we really are blind to it! The only person who can help us to see a blind spot is someone else. A wife can be good at seeing a blind spot her husband has, and a husband can do the same with his wife, but often neither are accurate because it usually takes some disassociated person to genuinely see what the person concerned cannot, or will not see.

We are prone to be subjective and too close to our own problems to see a cause. I would be delighted to give a simple formula to this problem but there is no easy answer. There are, however, principles that we can learn and apply.

Many adverse experiences in life are unquestionably allowed by God when there has been no personal failure on our part. We read in the scriptures how Jesus and His disciples were walking past a man who was blind from birth. The disciples asked Jesus this question:

> ' "*Rabbi, who sinned, this man or his parents, that he was born blind?*"
> "*Neither this man nor his parents sinned,*" *said Jesus,* "*but this happened so that the work of God might be displayed in his life.*" ' (John 9:2–3)

The natural tendency of the disciples was to find a cause for the blindness and their immediate reaction was to think that there had been some failure either by the man or his parents. That was very much in line with the Jewish thinking of those times. Jesus, however, completely squashed such a proposition and in fact was emphatic that neither the man nor his parents were at fault, but God had allowed this man to go through years of blindness so that the work of God might be displayed in his life.

It is hard to be objective regarding ourselves and difficult to realize that we all have some 'blind spots'.

The Book of Job gives us a similar situation. We read in the opening chapter of this book:

> '*Then the Lord said to Satan, "Have you considered my servant Job? There is no one on earth like him; he is blameless and upright, a man who fears God and shuns evil."*
> *"Does Job fear God for nothing?" Satan replied.*
> *"Have you not put a hedge around him and his household and everything he has? You have blessed the work of his hands, so that his flocks and herds are spread throughout the land.*
> *But stretch out your hand and strike everything he has, and he will curse you to your face."*
> *The Lord said to Satan, "Very well, then, everything he has is in your hands, but on the man himself do not lay a finger."*'
> (Job 1:8–12)

Later, God allowed Satan to attack Job's body and he was covered with painful sores, but in all of this Job did not sin in what he said. Job had done nothing wrong when God allowed this destruction and loss of family, possessions, and health to be inflicted upon him. God allowed a great test to come on Job, but in later years God restored to Job double of what he had had before these disasters came. God was allowing these extreme tests to prove the character of his servant Job.

Many adverse experiences of life are unquestionably allowed by God when there has been no personal failure on our part.

The Trial of Faith

I want to remind you of the suffering, testing, and trials of the apostle Paul. When writing to the Corinthian church he recounted what he had endured:

> *'Are they servants of Christ? (I am out of my mind to talk like this.) I am more. I have worked much harder, been in prison more frequently, been flogged more severely, and been exposed to death again and again,*
> *Five times I received from the Jews the forty lashes minus one.*
> *Three times I was beaten with rods, once I was stoned, three times I was shipwrecked, I spent a night and a day in the open sea, I have been constantly on the move. I have been in danger from rivers, in danger from bandits, in danger from my own countrymen, in danger from Gentiles; in danger in the city, in danger in the country, in danger at sea; and in danger from false brothers.*
> *I have laboured and toiled and have often gone without sleep; I have known hunger and thirst and have often gone without food; I have been cold and naked.*

Besides everything else, I face daily the pressure of my concern for all the churches.'

(2 Corinthians 11:23–28)

Were these experiences because Paul, the great apostle, did not know how to appropriate the benefits of what Christ had provided through the Cross? Did this man to whom Jesus gave the revelation of the church – a mystery that had been hidden down through the ages – not know how to receive the fullness of what Jesus had accomplished? Such a possibility is unthinkable, although some supposed faith teachers today would try to have us believe that if Paul knew as much as they do today, or had the faith that they claim to have, he would not have needed to face such hardships!

Was Paul suffering because he had sown negatively in his life? We are aware that Paul, before his conversion, was a persecutor of the church and a witness to the death of Stephen, the first martyr, but in receiving Christ he would have been totally forgiven. These sufferings that Paul experienced could not have been a result of reaping negatively from sowing disobedience! Paul was totally committed to the gospel of Jesus Christ. He challenged the Christians of his day to imitate him! Not many of us would dare to make such a claim.

The only other explanation is that God was moulding a man's life and character for the purpose that He required. God was taking a life that He had chosen and allowing him to go through the most harrowing experiences so that Paul would be equipped to accomplish all that the Lord wanted from his life. We don't usually learn much from the easy events of life. We learn when the pressures come and we have our backs to the wall and have to trust Jesus when we can't see the final result, and when apparent disaster stares us in the face. Paul's own fervent prayer was this:

> *'But whatever was to my profit I now consider loss for the sake of Christ. What is more, I consider everything a loss compared to the surpassing greatness of knowing Christ Jesus my Lord, for whose sake I have lost all things. I consider them rubbish, that I may gain Christ and be found in him, not having a righteousness of my own that comes from the law, but that which is through faith in Christ – that righteousness that comes from God and is by faith.*
>
> *I want to know Christ and the power of his resurrection and the fellowship of sharing in his sufferings, becoming like him in his death, and so, somehow, to attain to the resurrection from the dead.*
>
> *Not that I have already obtained all this, or have already been made perfect, but I press on to take hold of that for which Christ Jesus took hold of me.'*
>
> (Philippians 3:7–12)

God was moulding a man's life and character for the purpose that He required.

It is clear from the letters that Paul wrote to the different churches that he had many detractors in his day. It would be reasonable to assume that there were many in the church at that time who would have interpreted Paul's trials and sufferings to be the result of some personal disobedience or failure. Paul had many enemies within the church and often found it necessary to defend his apostleship. Those who were against him no doubt would have been pleased to point the finger of accusation at him because of his trials and hardships.

As we look back over the record of Paul's life and his effectiveness, fruitfulness, steadfastness, dedication, and the revelations he had received from the Lord, we see a man who may not have been perfect in everything he did, but one who was totally committed to the Lord Jesus Christ, and whose ministry evidenced signs, wonders, and the power of God. We see a man who, because of the testings and trials of life, became so strong that nothing could move him. Paul made these two different affirmations in two separate letters that he wrote to the churches:

> *'For our light and momentary troubles are achieving for us an eternal glory that far outweighs them all.*
> *So we fix our eyes not on what is seen, but on what is unseen. For what is seen is temporary, but what is unseen is eternal.'*   (2 Corinthians 4:17–18)

> *'Not only so, but we also rejoice in our sufferings, because we know that suffering produces perseverance; perseverance, character; and character, hope.*
> *And hope does not disappoint us, because God has poured out his love into our hearts by the Holy Spirit, whom he has given us.'*   (Romans 5:3–5)

The scriptures are clear; persecution, suffering, and testing are part of the true Christian life! In the Sermon on the Mount, Jesus said:

> *'Blessed are you when people insult you, persecute you and falsely say all kinds of evil against you because of me.*

Rejoice and be glad, because great is your reward in heaven, for in the same way they persecuted the prophets who were before you.' (Matthew 5:11–12)

Jesus predicted persecution for those who followed Him. It would be easy for someone to say, 'I am suffering and going through this difficult time because I am living in obedience to Jesus!' That may or may not be so. We are quick to find excuses for ourselves. There are, however, the three alternatives that could apply, and we must be very honest as we come to discern the cause of different problems.

The apostle Paul was experiencing an affliction at one time during his ministry and he prayed and asked the Lord to remove it. The reply he received was not what he would have expected, and he wrote about it in this way:

'To keep me from becoming conceited because of these surpassingly great revelations, there was given me a thorn in my flesh, a messenger of Satan, to torment me.
Three times I pleaded with the Lord to take it away from me.
But he said to me, "My grace is sufficient for you, for my power is made perfect in weakness." Therefore I will boast all the more gladly about my weaknesses, so that Christ's power may rest on me.
That is why, for Christ's sake, I delight in weaknesses, in insults, in hardships, in persecutions, in difficulties. For when I am weak, then I am strong.'
(2 Corinthians 12:7–10)

> *We see a man who, because of the testings and trials of life, became so strong that nothing could move him.*

There is no evidence in the Bible to suggest that Paul was referring to a physical sickness when he wrote of this *'thorn in the flesh.'* Paul may have been referring to the persecution, opposition and hardship that he constantly faced. It would be natural for Paul to pray earnestly for the Lord to deliver him out of such circumstances. On the other hand, there is no evidence to show that he was not suffering from a physical condition that may have made his missionary work more difficult. Any comment as to the meaning of Paul's *'thorn in the flesh'* is speculation. The heart of the meaning of this passage of scripture has to do with the response that Paul made to the Lord's reply to the prayer.

Paul accepted that the Lord was not going to remove the problem at that point in time. When Christ said, *'My grace is sufficient for you, for my power is made perfect in weakness,'* Paul accepted that answer without further question. Paul could have given up his missionary work! He could have become offended with Jesus because he didn't get what he would have liked! He could have lost confidence in the call that was on his life! He did not do any of these things! He pressed on with his work knowing that the Lord would give him the strength and power that he needed.

This is the acid test, to determine if God is allowing a problem for our growth and development and not because of some personal failure. Can we say in the midst of the difficulty that His grace is sufficient for us and that His power is made perfect in our time of weakness?

Trusting But Not Being Delivered

Life has its ups and downs and problems. I read this statement, 'Pain is inevitable, but misery is optional!' (Johnson, Barbara. *Pain is Inevitable but Misery is Optional*. Word Publishing: Eng. 1991). If we are in the midst of trouble, can we honestly say that the Lord's grace is sufficient for us, or are we so in despair that we are ready to give up? Obviously, the apostle Paul was desperate when he prayed to the Lord, and although this attack of Satan was not immediately removed, the promise of the Lord's help in the problem was enough for Paul to press on without wavering.

In Hebrews 11 we read of the great heroes of faith. Amazing conquests through faith, miracles, and victories are recorded. We read of men such as Enoch, Noah, Abraham, Isaac, Jacob, Joshua, Gideon, Samson, David, and others who through faith conquered kingdoms, administered justice, gained what had been promised, shut the mouths of lions, quenched the fury of the flames, and escaped the edge of the sword. The scripture says, 'Whose weakness was turned to strength' (Hebrews 11:32–34).

But as we read on in this chapter we come to an entirely different story:

> '... *Others were tortured and refused to be released, so that they might gain a better resurrection.*
> *Some faced jeers and flogging, while still others were chained and put in prison.*

172

> *They were stoned, they were sawed in two; they were*
> *put to death by the sword. They went about in sheep-*
> *skins and goatskins, destitute, persecuted and ill-*
> *treated – the world was not worthy of them.*
> *They wandered in deserts and mountains, and in caves*
> *and holes in the ground.'* (Hebrews 11:35–38)

What happened to these people? Were they disobedient or unable to reach God in prayer? Were they reaping
what they had sown? Do we have in Hebrews 11 a list of
successes who knew how to exercise faith and pray
through to a place of victory in their circumstances, and
also a group of failures who were disobedient and whose
prayers were unheard? Verse 39 in this chapter gives a
very clear answer:

> *'These were all commended for their faith, yet none of*
> *them received what had been promised.'*
> (Hebrews 11:39)

These were all commended for their faith, as well as
those who had had miraculous deliverances. They were
not suffering because of their inability to trust God, nor
were they reaping negatively from what they had sown,
but God had allowed them to suffer and even die!

No one is able to explain the ways of God. Why God
allows different events to take place, even to those who
love and serve Him with total trust, is known only to
God Himself. But we can be assured that every experience of life is allowed by the Lord so that if we make
right responses we will be prepared not only for God's
best in this life, but also in eternity.

> *Can we say in the midst of the difficulty that*
> *His grace is sufficient for us and that His*
> *strength is being revealed in our time of*
> *weakness?*

Opportunity Lost

By way of contrast, let us consider King Herod who was the only man in the Bible to whom Jesus refused to speak. What a distinction! There is no record of Jesus being unwilling to speak to any other person including prostitutes, publicans, lepers, scribes or Pharisees. Sometimes Jesus spoke sternly and with rebuke, but His words always contained hope and opportunity for reconciliation with God. To Herod, however, Jesus would not speak. Luke records this incident in his gospel:

> *'When Herod saw Jesus, he was greatly pleased,*
> *because for a long time he had been wanting to see*
> *him. From what he had heard about him, he hoped to*
> *see him perform some miracle.'* (Luke 23:8)

We could well think this would have been a great opportunity for Jesus to convince King Herod, a prominent national leader, that He had supernatural power and was the Son of God, but the scripture says:

> *'He plied him with many questions, but Jesus gave*
> *him no answer.'* (Luke 23:9)

Jesus refused to speak to Herod. There were no words of compassion or hope for this evil king and later Herod

174

reaped what he had sown as a result of a life of selfishness, brutality, and murder. God's temporal judgment upon Herod was recorded in chapter five of this book.

Another illustration concerns Judas, one of the twelve disciples, a man who was wonderfully favoured by God and given the privilege of being with Jesus for more than three years, and yet for his own selfish reasons accepted thirty pieces of silver to betray Jesus. Later, Judas, filled with despair and condemnation, hanged himself. Here was a man with one of the greatest opportunities of all history, but because of his greed and self-desire, he had reaped what he had sown.

Every experience of life is allowed by God so that, if we will make the right responses, we will be prepared not only for God's best in time, but also in eternity.

Dictator or Directed?

We are still examining how we can determine what is happening when there are problems and difficulties in our lives. It is hard when we are personally involved and are caught in despair. The Bible makes two special provisions to help us out of the dilemma in which we may find ourselves. The scriptures provide for the operation of spiritual authority and also for the plurality of leadership. The Bible tells us to submit to those who are over us:

'Obey your leaders and submit to their authority. They keep watch over you as men who must give an

> *account. Obey them so that their work will be a joy, not a burden, for that would be of no advantage to you.'*
> (Hebrews 13:17)

The Bible also says:

> *'Submit to one another out of reverence for Christ.'*
> (Ephesians 5:21)

Submission is a subject that has been misused and misunderstood. Submission is an attitude rather than an action. The New Testament does not provide that any person should be under the domination of another as our life relationship is essentially with the Lord Jesus Christ. But God has provided a way of protection by our being submitted to spiritual leaders and also to one another.

Submission is not to crush a person's life or to take away incentive, but that others would be able to give us objective discernment and counsel when we are confronted with the problems of life. This is also the reason for plurality of leadership so that no one man can take a dictatorial oversight.

God gives spiritual protection when we obey spiritual principles. We might wonder if an eldership, overseer, or pastor would always have the right answer for our lives, and of course each person has a right to express his own view point or leading in any situation. But if we will obey spiritual principles then, in the event of an overseer being wrong in his direction, God will still honour His principles and protect us even when we don't understand how He will do it.

I do not suggest that any person should violate his own conscience or act contrary to a genuine conviction in order to obey a spiritual authority. Generally speaking, we are safer obeying spiritual overseers, even if we think they are wrong, than doing what we want to do even if we think that we are right. Quite often right and wrong cannot be determined at the time an event is taking place and only time shows what was the correct course of action. Never overlook God's ability to intervene on behalf of the person who is acting with a sincere heart. These comments are made in regard to guidance or problems that are being faced and where it would be wise and beneficial to seek confirmation or counsel from an experienced leader or another mature Christian before taking some unilateral action.

God has provided a way of protection by our being submitted to spiritual authority and to one another.

When there is a dictatorial leader, there is none to whom he is accountable; there is none to give him correction so the New Testament pattern is very clearly that of elders: plural.

Perhaps you believe this and would say, 'Yes, I believe that the New Testament pattern for church government is plurality of leadership and that eldership is God's pattern. There should not be one man with all the say, dominating the life of the church, or a particular part of Christ's Body.' Do we realize, however, that while we may agree with this principle that it is easy to make ourselves a dictatorial authority over our own life? We say, 'No one tells me what to do. I can go straight to Jesus. I don't need a shepherd. I'm complete in Christ and don't need anybody else!' There is a degree of truth in those statements, but we can make ourselves a dictator over our own life by this attitude.

We must balance the amazing provision of personal relationship with Christ with the command that we are to submit to those having authority over us and also to one another. By submission, we allow God to protect us by the concern and counsel of leadership, and also by our brothers and sisters in Christ. They can help us to evaluate the circumstances in which we find ourselves. We can be sincere Bible-believing Christians and yet still need help when it comes to really discerning what is happening at any stage of our life.

We are safer obeying spiritual oversight even if we think they are wrong, than doing what we want even if we think we are right.

We need to understand the way that God's principles work. At creation God demanded obedience from Adam and placed Adam in authority over Eve. The purpose of God was that they should multiply and replenish the earth and rule over it. Eve failed in her submission to Adam and Adam failed in his obedience to God and they lost the opportunity to fulfil God's purpose. Had each done what had been required of them, they would have shared the rights that God had promised.

Jesus came as the last Adam, and completely fulfilled His task by obedience to the Father. Eve was a bride – a type of the church – so the church is to be in submission to her heavenly Bridegroom, Jesus. When the church is submitted to Christ the Head, then He brings His Bride to a place of equality so she rules and reigns with Him on the throne.

The Bible says that the husband is the head of the wife and that the wife is to submit to her husband. Christ is, of course, the head of the husband and the husband must obey the Lord. If the husband obeys Christ and the wife submits to her husband then God's divine order is complete, and they together, husband and wife, enter into equal rights in God and rule over the family.

Submission does not make one less than another. Submission in divine order, completes God's plan of authority, and allows equality, in sharing the rights and privileges as co-heirs with Christ. The fact that some leaders have misused the principle of submission and have brought people into bondage and dependence on them does not invalidate the truth of genuine Bible submission. Do not be afraid of biblical submission as it can be the means of releasing a person into liberty, and also a right understanding of God's will for his life.

At the time of writing this book one young woman in the church where I was pastor, gave me this unsolicited testimony:

> An incident occurred in my life some years ago during a time of rather bitter disillusionment and I had made a decision to leave the church. I thought to myself, 'I'll still believe in God but I won't go to church anymore.' When Sunday came, a small voice within me seemed to say, 'The pastor has been good to you. At least you can have the courtesy to tell him that you are going to leave.' I thought about it and decided that I would do that, so I dressed for church, arrived late and sat in the back and not near the front where I normally sat. God was merciful to me and I sensed His presence and suddenly thought, 'I don't care what people have done to me

or what they might do in the future or even what I have done myself, I love God and I am going to follow Him.' Something happened inside me!

Continuing her testimony, the young woman said that at the close of the service I had come to her and said, 'Where have you been?' Although she had been absent for seven weeks she said, 'Oh, I've just been thinking,' and I said to her, 'Can't you do that at church?' She said, 'No, this place affects my thinking too much,' and I replied, 'You have been taking a wrong course of action!' She continued with her story:

This was the end of a crisis for me. I never stayed away from church after that and when I thought about the incident it frightened me how closely I had come to really missing out in my walk with God. If I had not obeyed that little voice within me that sent me back to tell what I had intended doing, I would have left the church and I do not know what the consequences would have been. At the time I did not see any spiritual principle behind what had happened and thought to myself, 'How could God let my life hang on what seemed such a simple issue?' It was not, however, a simple issue; it was one that could have seriously affected my whole life. I now understand that God was protecting me and bringing me back under a spiritual overseer.

Submission, in divine order, completes God's plan of authority, and allows equality, in sharing the rights and privileges as co-heirs with Christ.

Do not underestimate the capacity of a believer in Christ to receive clear individual guidance by the Holy Spirit or to be led by the Word of God and prayer, but I want to stress that it is not always easy to genuinely hear from God in our Spirit. We need to learn to discern the voice of the Holy Spirit as distinct from our own spirit, and guidance and help from those who care for us is vital as we are developing in this ability.

The words, 'God has told me,' do not validate the actions of a person! So often a person has said to me, 'God has told me,' but the outcome has disproved the words, as the action taken by the person has resulted in confusion, disorder, and sometimes disaster. The mere expression, 'God has told me,' is not a divine seal on a course of action. Time has often proven that what was done by a person was his own desire and not guidance by the Holy Spirit.

Don't become a dictator over your own life! God wants us increasingly to learn how to discern His voice, but many factors are involved. Our conscience must be cleansed and kept sensitive. We must develop an intuitive ability to hear the inner voice of the Spirit of God and build ourselves up in the Word and in prayer. All of this can take time and experience, so keep a submissive attitude towards those who are in positions of delegated authority.

I had been a Christian for more than thirty years before I really discovered the importance of conscience in hearing the voice of God. I do not recall having heard a sermon or being given teaching on this subject in all that time. Often the comment had been passed, 'Do not trust your conscience; it is unreliable!'

From a careful study of scripture, I came to see that

181

our conscience was a vital faculty of the human spirit by which we could discern right or wrong and truth or error. In addition, our conscience is the God-ordained provision to enable us to discern the law of God which is actually written in our hearts.

The words, 'God has told me,' do not validate the actions of a person.

This subject is a matter for separate study, but let me say that because of sin and disobedience, man's conscience has been corrupted and calloused so as to greatly reduce its sensitivity. This, however, can be changed! The blood of Jesus Christ not only cleanses us from sin, but also cleanses our conscience from acts that lead to death (Hebrews 9:14).

When our conscience is spiritually cleansed as a result of the new birth, and kept sensitive by obedience to its promptings, then it becomes a vital factor to enable us to clearly hear the voice of God.

So many Christians fail at the basic levels of obedience, particularly in regard to reading of the Bible, prayer, and keeping a clear conscience. I have never in all my years of ministry dealt with a backslider who could honestly say, 'I have diligently read the Bible and prayed.'

Our communion with God is so vital to building and maintaining an ability to know clearly the direction of God. People can so glibly say that God has led them in a particular direction, but the evidence of their lives is one of self-pleasing and disorder. Any sincere person who considers that the Holy Spirit has given guidance in some important matter or direction should be willing to submit that guidance to trusted spiritual leaders for confirmation.

Over the years I have been glad to work with teams of men with whom I have been able to submit what I believed God was saying to the church, to the wider fellowship of churches, or to my life at a personal level. We can easily develop personal desires and convictions that may not be the will of God, and to have those who love and care for us say, 'We do not believe that this is the right action' is a valuable protection.

I came to see that our conscience was a vital faculty of the human spirit by which we could discern right and wrong, and truth and error.

A Mind Made Up!

The majority of people who have come to me for guidance over many years, particularly in matters of importance, have, generally speaking, already made up their own minds before coming. They have come to me for a 'rubber stamp' endorsement! The moment I have begun to question them or raised doubts as to their action there has been a reaction, and often they have been offended. Sometimes these people have then left the church!

It is easy to say spiritual words, but when we are confronted with the question of what is happening in life we need to realize that we are often the author of our own misfortune, because we will not act in accordance with God's way. Tragic results, backsliding, confusion, and resentment have followed those who have determined to go their own way.

I think with sadness of a group of people in one of the home meetings in my own church who left the church with a wrong attitude and without explanation. Within a comparatively short time hardly any were continuing as active Christians, yet all of them obviously thought that they were taking the right action in leaving the church. Time proved that the steps taken were of their own initiative and not of God's leading.

There is a continual heartache to pastors and loss to the Kingdom of God because men and women have made up their own mind and are determined to take action under the guise of God's will.

Tragic results, backsliding, confusion and resentment have followed those who have determined to go their own way.

On one occasion I listened to an international speaker teaching about the principle of release. He said that when we violate God's Word or way there is a bondage that can remain in our lives. He spoke particularly in regard to people leaving a church without making an explanation, or with hurt feelings and a critical spirit. The fact that they had been part of the local body for several years was totally immaterial to them, but because of some disagreement, they found it convenient to say that the Lord had told them to go.

This international speaker confided that on one occasion he had left the church where he had been the pastor because a set of hurtful circumstances and ill-will and bitterness had been involved. Ultimately, he returned to that church and stood before the congregation and asked them to release him because he had found, that in the manner of his leaving the church, he had brought restriction upon his own life and ministry. He had been unable to find freedom and peace in God because he had violated God's way of being guided by the Holy Spirit and confirmation from others. Incidents similar to this, by either leadership or lay people, arise so often in church life that we need to face the truth that confusion and problems will follow us if we act in selfishness and haste.

Let us be very clear about two matters:

1. If we do not appropriate what Christ has provided for us we are committing sin!

By continuing with old attitudes of mind, emotion, and will, we reduce the power of Christ's death and resurrection to bring us into complete liberty and victory. There are several different Greek words that are translated by the English word 'sin'. One of these words is *'hamartia'* which means, 'to fall short of the mark or target'. This is the word used by the writer to the Hebrew church where he says:

> *'Therefore, since we are surrounded by such a great cloud of witnesses, let us throw off everything that hinders and the sin that so easily entangles, and let us run with perseverance the race marked out for us.'*
>
> (Hebrews 12:1)

The sin that easily entangles us is the sin to fail to be all that we could be, and not to accept all that Christ has provided. It is easy to be satisfied with the mediocre and fail to attain the full purpose of God for our lives. If we live our own way, doing those things we did before coming to Christ, and continue with old habits, then we are committing sin by failing to 'hit the target' God has set for us.

We need to consider not only violations of God's Word but also failure to press on to God's will for our lives.

---

2. If we sow any form of unrighteousness or disobedience as Christians it is sin!

We thank God for His willingness to forgive, but if we disobey His Word it is sin. So we become accountable, and the result will be the reaping of a negative harvest. Remember that a harvest is always greater in proportion than that which is sown. One seed seldom brings forth one; it brings forth many.

We need to consider not only violations of God's Word but also failure to press on to fulfil God's will for our lives. Both of these aspects are vital if we are to avoid God's judicial dealings.

Signs and Symptoms

How can we know the cause of the problem or difficulty through which we are passing? In the medical profession doctors look for signs and symptoms to help their diagnosis. It is possible to make a spiritual diagnosis.

What are the signs and symptoms if our difficulty is due to failure to appropriate all the provisions of the Cross or if we are reaping negative results in our lives from sin or disobedience?

If we are reaping adverse results because we have sown negatively, then there will be in our lives a sense of despair, doubt, confusion, and fear. There will be times of unbelief and a sense of great pressure. There will be a heaviness upon our lives and a lack of strength. Not all of these will be present together, but we will experience some if not all of these until the right action is taken to bring freedom and release. In Psalm 33, King David writing of his experience following his sin, made the statement that is recorded in The Living Bible in this manner:

> *'But my dishonesty made me miserable, and filled my days with frustration. All day and all night, Your hand was heavy on me. My strength evaporated like water on a sunny day.'* (Psalm 32:3–4)

David was reaping from what he had sown, and this was evident by the signs and symptoms that were affecting his life.

We have looked at the two negative aspects – failing to appropriate or reaping what we have sown – so it is now essential that we learn to clearly understand if our difficulties are being allowed by God for our growth and development.

What are the signs and symptoms if we are being disciplined, or 'pruned' by God so that we will be true sons and daughters and be able to bring forth more fruit? We will have a great sense of confidence in God and a recognition of the sufficiency of His grace. Even in the midst of turmoil, there will be inner peace and joy. We will have a clear conscience and be free of inner guilt because of what we were once trying to hide. There will be an acceptance that God is working all things together for good. We will not have to talk ourselves into believing this, but we will know it deep in our spirits and will have confidence that in spite of all that is taking place, God is still in control and has not forsaken us.

We will know what it means to be an overcomer and so rise above the circumstances that confront us, and not only win victory over them, but continue to conquer them until they have no active power to rise up again and bring despair to us. This is what the Bible means when it speaks about our being *'more than conquerors'* (Romans 8:37). Not only have we conquered, but we have also subdued the enemy or area of failure, and it has no power to affect us again.

Even in the midst of turmoil, there will be an inner peace and joy.

The inner witness of the Holy Spirit is a great confidence, but we need to have this confirmed by our brothers and sisters in Christ. It is possible to convince ourselves that we have peace even when we are wrong. There is a significant passage of scripture found in Deuteronomy following the promises of blessings or curses that are given for obedience or disobedience:

> *'When such a person hears the words of this oath, he invokes a blessing on himself and therefore thinks, "I will be safe, even though I persist in going my own way." This will bring disaster on the watered land as well as the dry.*
> *The Lord will never be willing to forgive him; his wrath and zeal will burn against that man. All the curse written in this book will fall upon him, and the Lord will blot out his name from under heaven.'*
>
> (Deuteronomy 29:19–20)

This is a very solemn passage that speaks of a man who is violating the Word of God and yet blesses himself in his heart and says that he will have peace. People have sometimes said to me, 'I have a perfect peace about what I am doing,' but later events have proven beyond doubt that their action was wrong. The Living Bible perhaps gives even a clearer understanding of the verses to which we have just referred:

> *'Let no one blithely think, when he hears the warnings of this curse, I shall prosper even though I walk in my own stubborn way! For the Lord will not pardon! His anger and jealousy will be hot against that man. And all the curses written in this book shall lie heavily upon him, and the Lord will blot out his name from under heaven.'* (Deuteronomy 29:19–20)

It is not only our own inner peace and confidence that is needed, it is also the confirmation of those who can look at our attitude and action objectively. From years of observing Christians, and from my own personal experience, I am convinced that a high percentage of our problems are of our own making. We are under the judicial dealings of God because of some disobedience or failure even though we have been forgiven. Let us look at some confirming scriptures:

> *'Have you noticed how Ahab has humbled himself before me? Because he has humbled himself I will not bring this disaster in his day, but I will bring it on his house in the days of his son.'* (1 Kings 21:29)

Because Ahab humbled himself, God removed the immediate judgment from him, but later allowed the penalty to come on Ahab's household. God extended mercy to Ahab, but not removal of the consequences. We read:

> *'Because your heart was responsive and you humbled yourself before the Lord when you heard what I have spoken against this place and its people, that they would become accursed and laid waste, and because you tore your robes and wept in my presence, I have heard you, declares the Lord.'* (2 Kings 22:19)

This is an incident in the life of King Josiah when God spared him because of his youth, but later the nation suffered because of his sin.

It is possible to convince ourselves that we have peace, even when we are in the wrong.

> *'When the Lord saw that they humbled themselves, this word of the Lord came to Shemaiah: "Since they have humbled themselves, I will not destroy them but will soon give them deliverance. My wrath will not be poured out on Jerusalem through Shishak.*
> *They will, however, become subject to him, so that they may learn the difference between serving me and serving the kings of other lands."'*
> (2 Chronicles 12:7–8)

This passage speaks of King Rehoboam who repented of the sin he had committed, but the Bible says that although he received mercy from God and deliverance in his immediate situation, he went on reaping some of the consequences of his folly.

> *'Then Hezekiah repented of the pride of his heart, as did the people of Jerusalem; therefore the Lord's wrath did not come upon them during the days of Hezekiah.'*
>
> (2 Chronicles 32:26)

Hezekiah, after his failure, humbled himself and God removed the punishment that had been threatened, but later the nation suffered.

Sometimes we can escape the consequences of our actions but leave a negative heritage for others. The Bible says that the sins of the fathers can be visited upon the children to the third and fourth generations! (Exodus 20:5).

When God is allowing testing for our development, however, we will not be like these Old Testament figures who wilfully disobeyed and then sought God's mercy, but we will have an attitude of submission and humility. We will not be arrogant and self-willed, determined to do what we think is right regardless of the opinions of others who are concerned for our welfare. More tragedies have come from such an attitude than from any other single cause in the life of the church. Years of confusion have often followed those who have acted in this way. Jesus made this statement:

> *'The greatest among you will be your servant.*
> *For whoever exalts himself will be humbled, and whoever humbles himself will be exalted.'*
>
> (Matthew 23:11–12)

God asks for humility from us, then when we act this way he gives us honour and recognition. James says this:

191

'Humble yourselves before the Lord, and He will lift you up.' (James 4:10)

The apostle Peter continues with the same theme:

'Young men, in the same way be submissive to those who are older. All of you, clothe yourselves with humility toward one another, because, "God opposes the proud but gives grace to the humble."
Humble yourselves, therefore, under God's mighty hand, that He may lift you up in due time.'
(1 Peter 5:5–6)

God wants to honour us if we will be humble and submissive. When we maintain this attitude, then even though we pass through times that may seem difficult, God will use the circumstances to refine our character and cause us to grow more like Christ. This is, of course, God's ultimate purpose.

Sometimes we can escape the consequences of our action, but leave a negative heritage for others.

We can live in genuine freedom and have victory over the adverse circumstances which confront us. We can enjoy God's fellowship and peace through His forgiveness. We can have the confidence that because of God's pardon we are not suffering the consequences of sin. This is what God wants. He does not want people under condemnation and fear, but people who are filled with joy and peace and who are overflowing with hope, knowing that in every test the grace of God will be sufficient for them.

There are times when we all feel a measure of despair. I have often felt like giving up the responsibility of church leadership. I have never wanted to give up my faith in the Lord. I have never wanted to be a backslider. There have been, however, times of deep disappointment when I have been discouraged and later found it necessary to confess to the Lord that I had not been looking to Him but to the problem. Sometimes I have had to reap what I have sown and go through the dealings of God in a judgmental way because of my own fear, disobedience, or unwillingness to trust Him when I was under pressure. We all have the same human tendencies that cause us to feel the impact of opposition or hurts, but the Lord wants to teach us to stand fast and accept that all of these events will ultimately be for our good.

When conducting a series of studies on the Sermon on the Mount, I was impressed by the words in the Lord's Prayer which make this simple statement, *'Give us today our daily bread'* (Matthew 6:11). What great faith it requires to be able to pray those words and ask for a supply sufficient for only one day! Not many of us would like to be in the position of having food for only one day in our house!

We can live in genuine freedom and have victory over the adverse circumstances which confront us.

What trust in God had to be shown by the people of Israel when wandering in the wilderness to gather only enough manna for one day! What natural doubts would have been in their minds wondering whether the supply would again be available the next day.

We may be faced with times when we will need an absolute assurance that God is with us in spite of opposition or hardship, so we need to know how to discern what is happening in our lives. If we apply the principles set out in this chapter, we will quickly learn whether we are suffering because of our own failure or are being trained as true sons and daughters of God.

'Since, then, you have been raised with Christ, set your hearts on things above, where Christ is seated at the right hand of God.

Set your minds on things above, not on earthly things.

For you died, and your life is now hidden with Christ in God.

When Christ, who is your life, appears, then you also will appear with him in glory.

Put to death, therefore, whatever belongs to your earthly nature: sexual immorality, impurity, lust, evil desires and greed, which is idolatry.

Because of these, the wrath of God is coming.

You used to walk in these ways, in the life you once lived.

But now you must rid yourselves of all such things as these: anger, rage, malice, slander and filthy language from your lips.

Do not lie to each other, since you have taken off your old self with its practices and have put on the new self, which is being renewed in knowledge in the image of its Creator....

Therefore, as God's chosen people, holy and dearly loved, clothe yourselves with compassion, kindness, humility, gentleness and patience.

Bear with each other and forgive whatever grievances you may have against one another. Forgive as the Lord forgave you.

And over all these virtues put on love, which binds them all together in perfect unity.

Let the peace of Christ rule in your hearts, since as members of one body you were called to peace. And be thankful.

Let the word of Christ dwell in you richly as you teach and admonish one another with all wisdom, and as you sing psalms, hymns and spiritual songs with gratitude in your hearts to God.'　　(Colossians 3:1–10 & 12–16)

Chapter 7

How to Forgive

We have examined many different aspects as we have studied the biblical basis of forgiveness, and I now want to give some practical ways by which we can achieve the object of knowing how to genuinely forgive.

Hearing or Doing?

It is not difficult to set out principles and commands that we discover in the Bible, but to put them into practice is, as all of us have discovered, an entirely different matter. We can know what the Bible says, we can agree with it, but when it comes to doing it, the challenge can be too hard for us.

Jesus knew that men and women were better hearers than doers and the Bible has much to say about the difference between hearing and doing. In particular, Jesus spoke strongly on the subject when He said to the crowd who had gathered, *'Do you have eyes but fail to see, and ears but fail to hear?'* (Mark 8:18). These people were watching Him and listening to Him, but obviously were not putting into practice what was being said. In Matthew 7 at the close of the chapter concluding the Sermon on the Mount, the Lord emphasized with a powerful parable the difference between hearing and doing. I have always been challenged by this parable of the two houses, one built on the sand and the other on the rock.

It is easy to tell people to be doers of the Word and not hearers only. This living out the Word of God must become real in our experience. We cannot just give lip service to what the Bible says; there must be a definite implementation of the scripture. We read:

> *'We know that God does not listen to sinners. He listens to the godly man who does his will.'*
>
> (John 9:31)

It is not merely our worshipping that causes God to hear us, but it is a worshipper who does His will that the Lord hears. The theme of being a doer and not a hearer only is repeated in many parts of scripture. We read this in the letter written by James:

> *'Anyone who listens to the word but does not do what it says is like a man who looks at his face in a mirror and, after looking at himself, goes away and immediately forgets what he looks like.*
> *But the man who looks intently into the perfect law that gives freedom, and continues to do this, not forgetting what he has heard, but doing it – he will be blessed in what he does.'*
> (James 1:23–25)

The difference between building upon a rock and building upon sand is not how much we know, or how much we believe, but how much we do.

The emphasis is upon the need to put into practice what we hear. James continues his letter with this statement:

> *'Anyone, then, who knows the good he ought to do and doesn't do it, sins.'*
> (James 4:17)

If we are aware of truth and do not do what is commanded, we are guilty not merely of an omission, but of sin! There are acts of commission where we deliberately violate God's Word, but there are also acts of omission, where we know to do what God commands but we fail to do it. Both are sins as far as God is concerned.

A Root Cause

The practical application of our faith very often seems too difficult. We can be extremely thankful that God forgives us, but we also need to be aware of our responsibility to forgive one another. We can also acknowledge that failure to forgive another person will impair our fellowship with God. We can accept the Bible statement that unforgiveness can cause a root of bitterness which can defile ourselves and many others, yet in spite of this knowledge we may have been so deeply hurt by the events of life that it seems impossible to forgive.

We must find a practical answer. How can we forgive when the hurts have been so deep and the wounds have done so much damage to our personality that we cannot put our knowledge into practice?

In the last chapter titled 'What is Happening?' we examined various causes of problems and turmoil that occur in peoples' lives. Were those difficulties a result of reaping what had been sown? Were they because of a failure to appropriate the provisions of the Cross? Or was God allowing us to be tested to build our character? The root problem, the very centre of the subject we are studying, is our failure to forgive others! Because we have not forgiven some other person, we are living with a major problem. Unforgiveness eats away at all areas of our lives mentally, emotionally, and spiritually, and is often the primary reason for our being miserable. Let me repeat what Jesus said:

> *'For if you forgive men when they sin against you, your heavenly Father will also forgive you.*
> *But if you do not forgive men their sins, your Father will not forgive your sins.'* (Matthew 6:14–15)

I said in the third chapter that this statement by Jesus could not possibly apply to the forgiveness that has to do with our eternal salvation, otherwise salvation would be in some measure of works and the grace of God would be undermined. Jesus was not speaking about salvation when He made that declaration.

On one occasion a prominent businessman spoke to me about the question of forgiveness and when I told him about my studies on the subject he said, 'For some time I have been very concerned about the statement in the Lord's Prayer where it says, *"Forgive us our debts, as we also have forgiven our debtors"*' (Matthew 6:12). This man attended a traditional church where it was the custom for the congregation to repeat the Lord's Prayer together. He continued, 'For some time now I have been unable to say those words as I have become so concerned about the implications of asking God to forgive me in proportion to how I forgive others.'

This man knew that his ability to forgive others did

not match the forgiveness that he needed from God, and so he was in confusion. I was able to tell him that I did not believe that the forgiveness referred to had to do with our eternal salvation, but with our fellowship with God and was, therefore, still a vital factor for our inner peace, emotional stability, and Christian growth.

If we do not forgive another person we do not lose our salvation, but it affects our relationship with God and in turn this can bring negative results physically, mentally, and emotionally in our own lives. And it happens!

How can we forgive when the hurts have been so deep and the wounds have done so much damage to our personality that we cannot put our knowledge into practice?

We must learn to forgive or we will constantly be at odds with God and ourselves. Our continuing intimate fellowship with God and the enjoyment of His daily presence is endangered if we will not forgive others. We may be saved, but we will certainly not enjoy the blessing, joy, health, strength and quickening of the Holy Spirit, because we have brought ourselves under God's judgmental dealings by violating one of His great principles.

We must remember that forgiveness by us does not condone the actions or words of another person. One of the reasons why people are reluctant to forgive is that they think that by forgiving they are endorsing a person's action. This is not so! What we are doing is leaving the judgment and the consequences of the other person's actions in the hands of an all-seeing and all-knowing God. We can have complete confidence that when we forgive, God goes on dealing with the problem and it is now His responsibility, not ours.

There are many hidden causes and reasons why people offend against others. I have tried to look objectively at different situations that have occurred in my own experience, but to know the heart of another person is impossible.

Each of us takes a certain action because we think we have a valid cause, and others may not understand why we have done it. The heart of a man or a woman is known only to God. We will generally see events from our own point of view, so if I am involved in a situation where I have been hurt or offended, I will have a natural bias in my own favour. The only sensible action that we can take is to leave the matter to God who knows the heart of the other person and not just the outward circumstances that we see. By doing this we keep ourselves free from God's judgment, because we have genuinely forgiven the one who has offended us. Our fellowship with God is kept in harmony and the Lord takes care of the problem.

We must learn to forgive or we will constantly be at odds with God and ourselves.

Benefits to Receive

There are practical steps that we can take so that we will not be caught in the snare of unforgiveness. I suppose that hardly a week goes by without our being offended or hurt in some way, either at work, at home, or in church life. Nearly all of us are sensitive to what others say or do. Some pretend to be indifferent to hurtful

situations but often underneath, they are deeply
wounded, but are too proud to acknowledge it. It is natural to be hurt or offended when we are wrongly treated.
What is unnatural is not to care or to try and ignore it,
and that can result in a person becoming calloused and
bitter. We have to work hard at implementing the clear
principles which we find in the Bible, but if we don't we
will find ourselves holding unforgiveness and will suffer
the consequences.

Let me give some definite steps that we can take:

Remind yourself of the benefits you will receive spiritually, mentally, emotionally and physically, by genuinely forgiving others. This is the first step.

We are not selfish in doing this. Take into account the
beneficial results if you forgive, or the harmful results if
you do not forgive. The 'old self life' loves to hold on to
its hurts! We say, 'I'm not going to let that pass without
retaliation. I won't forget that easily.' That is 'self'
speaking. We are in a battle against our old nature and
we must remind ourselves of the blessings that God gives
when we act and respond His way. In John's third letter
he says:

> *'Dear friend, I pray that you may enjoy good health
> and that all may go well with you, even as your soul is
> getting along well.'* (3 John:2)

That is God's desire. Remind yourself that the Lord
wants the best for you. There are great benefits to be
received in every area of life if we will do what God says
and honestly forgive those who may have wronged us.
Unforgiveness will rob you of the best.

Take into account the beneficial results if you forgive, or the harmful results if you do not forgive.

Forgiveness Received

Remember that you have been forgiven by God. This is the second step.

All of us were sinners without hope and deserving of nothing except death and eternal separation from God. The Lord in His great love sent Jesus, allowing Him to be despised, rejected, crucified, and taking the sin of us all. In this action God forgave us in Christ.

Remember the forgiveness that you have received. Not only what we have received but what we continue to receive as we confess and repent if there is further failure. Could any of us say that even in a short period of time we had not violated God's Word, His way, or His goal for our life? We may not have deliberately sinned, but perhaps in some unguarded moment we missed an opportunity for good, yet God forgave! You may have said, 'Lord I'm sorry! I didn't really mean to do that! I was indifferent! I was lazy! Please forgive me!' And God forgave. If we receive forgiveness on this scale, it is a small thing to forgive others even if they don't ask for forgiveness.

Keep thanking the Lord for His willingness to forgive. I have always appreciated God's mercy. The mercy of God has been an attribute of His nature which has blessed and encouraged me. In spite of all our failure God is merciful, and of course, mercy leads to forgiveness and forgiveness to pardon. We need to have an attitude of thankfulness to God that, in spite of our failure, weakness, or discouragement, He has forgiven and restored us to fellowship. If we do this we will find that it is another practical way of helping us to forgive others. We will keep sensitive to the subject of forgiveness.

An Inviolate Principle

Recognize the inviolate principle of sowing and reaping. This is the third step.

We have already dealt with this subject in detail, but it is a truth which must constantly be kept in mind. Every action of ours will bring forth a definite result. This is unchanging. If we sow evil then sooner or later we will reap evil. If we sow that which is good we will reap positive benefits.

The results can vary according to how much attention we give to the seed we have sown. In the natural, when a seed is sown it requires watering and to be cared for in order to bring forth a full crop. If the seed is sown and then neglected and left without water, it might never germinate.

In the spiritual realm we might sow a seed and immediately realize its negative possibility and act instantly to destroy its power to bring forth a negative harvest. This is done by immediate repentance, confession, and, if applicable, restitution. Very seldom, however, do people do this, but they either allow the seed to lie and be watered by the general circumstances of life or they actively assist the development by continuing their negative course of action.

Keep thanking God for His willingness to forgive.

Let me give a personal experience that happened during the time that my wife and I were selling one property and purchasing another. One of the people who was interested in buying our property was a businessman. He came with his wife to inspect our home on several occasions and meticulously checked out every aspect of the premises. He drove his car into the garage to make sure that it would fit comfortably, and finally made an offer that was far below a fair market value. Without hesitation we turned down the the offer. The next day the agent handling the transaction telephoned and said, 'I've got another buyer that I am sure will purchase the property.' The person came and accepted the price that we had asked. Later the contract for the sale was signed. Within two days the original man telephoned and said, 'Have you signed the contract?' I said, 'Yes.' He replied, 'I'll give you $2,000 more if you'll get the buyer to change her mind.' I said, 'It's too late!'

This man had wanted to purchase the apartment we owned in this particular high-rise block, but because of his hard bargaining he had lost the opportunity. Later he purchased an apartment in the block but one without many of the advantages and extras which ours had, and he finally paid many thousands of dollars more. He sowed from a selfish spirit and reaped a loss.

I am not against someone looking for a good business deal, but there is a difference between being an astute businessman and seeking to deprive someone of a fair transaction. I use this illustration because it made an impact on me at the time and clearly illustrates that we will reap what we sow whether in business, spiritually, in home life or in other personal relationships. Take this principle seriously. It may not happen immediately and we may think that we are getting away with it, but we won't because 'the birds will come home to roost.' It is a principle of God's Word, not a theory.

It is essential that we forgive quickly. The longer we hold unforgiveness the harder it is to let go. The more we think about the reasons for our hurt and dwell upon it, the more our mind is captivated by the supposed justice of our case. Then we try to justify our attitude and are caught in the web of unforgiveness.

We will reap what we sow whether in business, spiritually, in home life or in other personal relationships.

We are strange people! We think about a hurt and it seems to get bigger and bigger, and we begin to think of what we could have said at the time the problem occurred. We think of a sharp retort that would have answered a cutting word, or a weakness in an accusation where a right word from us would have proved the person wrong. The more we think this way the larger the hurt grows until it has expanded out of all proportion.

Some years ago I read a story entitled 'Want to Borrow a Jack'. It told of a man who was driving his car on a country road at night and got a flat tyre. When he went to change the wheel he discovered that he had left the jack for the car at home. There he was, stranded on a lonely road in the darkness with no other cars passing by, with a flat tyre and no jack to change the wheel. He waited and waited, but no car came. In the distance he could see a light so he thought to himself, 'That is a farm house and the people will probably have a car. I'll walk there and ask to borrow a jack.' So he set off.

As he walked, he began to muse within himself and said, 'Well, perhaps they might not have a jack or might not like being disturbed at night. They will probably say to me, "If you are stupid enough to leave home without a jack, you can pay to hire it." I will say, "Pay to borrow a jack! I didn't deliberately get a flat tyre! Can't you help a man in time of need?"'

The imagined conversation continued. 'He will probably say, "It will cost you $20 if you want to use my jack." I will say, "$20 just to let me have a loan of a jack!"' The man looked up and suddenly the lights in the house went out. He thought, 'Now they are in bed! It will probably be worse! Now the farmer won't want to get out of bed and will probably say, "If I have to get out of bed to get a jack for you it will cost you $40."' The man angrily said to himself, '$40 just to borrow a jack!'

He walked aggressively to the front door of the house mumbling to himself, '$40 just to borrow a jack.' He knocked loudly on the door. An upstairs window opened and a man leaned out and said, 'Hello, what do you want?' The stranded traveller, angry and stirred by his own thoughts, looked up to the face in the window and shouted, 'You and your jack, you can keep it!!'

Isn't that true of human nature? We build up a big case about what might happen, or we feel resentful about a real hurt or the words someone used and what we should have said in return, and all the time we are enlarging the problem. If we have a need to forgive, let us act on it quickly.

It is essential that we forgive quickly. The longer we hold unforgiveness the harder it is to let go.

When my older brother first started work as a junior in a carpet warehouse, it was in the days when a company manager was a person to be feared, and this hard-headed manager said to my brother, 'I want to give you some advice; cultivate a good memory.' That sounded like wisdom, but it was what followed that was so significant. The manager said, 'If you don't have a good memory you might forget someone against whom you have a grudge!' Here was a man whose desire for a good memory was to make sure that he would continue to hold resentment and get even with others. That man died years later miserable, lonely, and largely friendless. How tragic! Learn to forgive quickly because we will never beat the principle of reaping what we sow.

Whose Life and Whose Work?

Realize that your life does not belong to you but to God. This is the fourth step. Paul wrote this:

> 'For none of us lives to himself alone and none of us dies to himself alone.
> If we live, we live to the Lord; and if we die, we die to the Lord. So, whether we live or die, we belong to the Lord.
> For this very reason, Christ died and returned to life so that he might be the Lord of both the dead and the living.'
> (Romans 14:7–9)

Our life is not our own! Is that statement a spiritual cliché or truth? Most of the reasons we have for holding unforgiveness relate to personal hurts. Children have been hurt by their parents perhaps through strict discipline, lack of love, neglect, or even abuse. Parents have been hurt by their children as a result of unthankfulness and indifference for all the provisions and sacrifices that have been made. Wives have been deserted by their husbands and left without financial support. Husbands may have been betrayed by their wives. The list is endless. Personal hurts are usually the cause of unforgiveness. Paul's letter to the Romans includes this statement:

> *'For we know that our old self was crucified with him so that the body of sin might be done away with, that we should no longer be slaves to sin.'* (Romans 6:6)

In the context, these words refer to sin, but they can equally apply to our personal rights. We do not have personal rights! The Bible makes clear that if our life belongs to Christ, then we do not have anything we can claim to be our own. If we were deserving of death because of sin, then our life is dependent entirely upon Christ. This truth must be constantly affirmed.

The problem both in the church and in our personal lives is that we know these words so it is easy to say them, but putting them into action can be a major battle. We must get to grips with this truth if we are going to win the battle to genuinely forgive. Acknowledge that you do feel hurt, but also acknowledge these truths, 'I am dead! My life is hidden with Christ in God! I live but only because I live in Him and He lives in me!' We do not have personal rights. Our lives belong to Christ.

> **It is because of personal hurts that there is usually unforgiveness in the hearts of people.**

Reassess that the spiritual work we are doing belongs to God and not ourselves. This is the fifth step.

If we are in some position of leadership, this is a particular area of challenge. Most Christians find that the greatest number of hurts and disappointments that arise in life do not come from people in their secular environment but from people in the church.

I was a self-employed businessman for twenty-five years, and although I suffered a certain amount of opposition and unjustified criticism in my business life I had to endure more ill-will, bitterness, disloyalty, and untruthfulness within church life. So often the hurts we receive and the problems we face come from those we love and care for rather than from the outsider.

This does not only happen in leadership! It is in any task that we do. Other people are unappreciative of what we have done. We may have laboured in some task, given sacrificial service, taught Sunday School, led a youth group or been involved in some other voluntary work, and nobody expressed appreciation but were to the contrary, critical. The task may have cost us money and time, yet all we received was criticism or lack of thanks. When we have experiences like these, the conditions for unforgiveness are present.

The last twenty-five years have produced some exciting spiritual progress. There has been the Charismatic Renewal, the introduction of church growth seminars and principles, and a recognition of the five-fold ministry gifts that Christ has given for the equipping of the church. But the current spiritual scene is still one of suspicion, misunderstanding, disloyalty, criticism, exaggeration, and sometimes hostility. We should rejoice at the good things that the Holy Spirit is doing, but conditions within the church and among believers constantly give rise to the need for forgiveness.

So often the hurts we receive and the problems we face come from those we love and care for rather than from the outsider.

How can we forgive when the very work of God in which we are involved is hindered and set back by the selfish actions of men and women? A church body that may have taken years to build is suddenly split by an associate and we say, 'How can we forgive someone who does that?' The answer is quite simple although it may be hard to put into operation when we are passing through the trauma. The fact is, it is not our work; it is the Lord's work. A church does not belong to a man or a woman or the eldership. The church belongs to Jesus Christ. Jesus said, *'I will build my church'* (Matthew 16:18).

God gives us the privilege of being co-workers with Christ, but it is the Lord's work. We are not building a personal kingdom. We are workers in the Kingdom of God and we need to remind ourselves of this. It is not a personal ministry that is at stake. We are servants of Christ, and God has a right to take up a person and use him or set him aside as He desires. It is the prerogative of the Lord to work within His church as He wishes. Often it is difficult to come to grips with this as we believe we have been called to a task and we see others bringing disruption and hurt to the body. The natural tendency is to fight back and to deal with the trouble-makers, but we must keep reminding ourselves that the work belongs to God and not to us.

That does not mean that we stand back and allow Satan to do whatever he wants. We must be on our guard, and be diligent and fervent in all we do. But when we have done all that we can righteously do, we must then leave God to do the rest.

God knows how to purge, refine, and build, so the moment we think it is our work and that the success of the church depends upon us and we are its protector, then we have a wrong perspective. It is God's work! When we realize this, then the weight of the hurts and burdens that give rise to unforgiveness and have come because of our desire to protect a work will lift from us.

Forgiveness Does Not Excuse!

Reassure yourself that forgiveness and pardon are not the same. This is the sixth step.

I have stressed this previously but I want to summarize it again. We do not have the responsibility to complete the moral cycle and see someone receive his just punishment. God knows all the facts without distortion or bias. The record of the Bible is clear; God will deal with every problem and do whatever is necessary for correction, so we can leave the judgment and consequences to Him.

It is the prerogative of the Lord to work within His church as He wishes.

We have considered six definite attitudes to adopt and actions to take in order to genuinely forgive. These are clear principles. Six positive steps we can take to help us to forgive; affirmations that we can make every day, if necessary, to overcome the problem of unforgiveness.

There is one other vital aspect that we must recognize. Jesus did not only say, 'Forgive one another' (Matthew 6:15). He also said, 'Love one another, even our enemies' (Matthew 5:44). This is another key in helping us to forgive someone who has let us down, wronged and hurt us, or even despised us. Yes, Jesus said we were to love even our enemies! Someone who has failed us does not automatically become our enemy, but we may find it impossible initially to have the same complete trust and confidence in a person who has let us down as we did before the problem arose. The Lord does not expect us to have the same confidence! A person must be proved again, and his integrity and credibility re-established.

Many people have an inaccurate understanding of trust. We put our trust in a friend or even in a family member, and that person fails the trust we put in him. It is almost certain that we will all fail some trust that is put in us. Someone confides in another and asks that the information not be given to any one else. A typical conversation goes like this, 'I have just heard some confidential news and if you promise not to tell anyone else, I will tell you.' Most of us are too curious to decline the opportunity to hear some hot gossip so we listen intently.

We now have the challenge to keep that information private. Information can represent power, and the only way we can exercise that power is to pass the news to another person. Of course, we only do so after exacting from them the promise not to tell anyone else! And so the news spreads and we have violated the original trust that was placed in us.

God knows how unreliable all of us can be, and the Bible actually tells us not to trust another person (Psalm 146:3). This may sound surprising as we are always looking for someone to trust, and we complain bitterly when someone fails us. It is true, however, that the Bible tells us to trust only God but to love one another. True love compensates for the weaknesses that are inevitable in men and women. While we do and must trust the motives of a loved-one we also know that the best of his intentions can fail, but true love makes allowances for failure.

A person must be proved again and his integrity and credibility re-established.

We do need some measure of confidence in people, and it is a blessing to have as our friends those who are usually reliable and who will protect us from the attacks of others. When someone has been in this category and has then failed you, it may take a little time to re-establish the same sense of confidence that you previously had, particularly if the failure has been repeated. But regardless of how often a person fails us, we still have the greater responsibility of loving him through Jesus Christ.

As mentioned earlier there is a common idea that because God is loving and forgiving, He forgets about failure. God never forgets! When the Bible speaks about God forgetting, it is used in the sense of His not inflicting a penalty that otherwise would be due. When the Bible says that God will no longer remember our sins and iniquities it does not mean that He cannot recall them any more, but that He does not hold them against us. The average human being is incapable of forgetting apart from the dimming of memory with the passage of time. But as God proves us after failure, so we must prove people when they have failed us, and at the same time we have a clear responsibility to forgive them according to scripture (Matthew 18:21–22).

Loving and Liking

From what we have already seen in the scripture, it is obvious that we must be able to both love and forgive a person, even when we do not have the same complete confidence in him. There is a difference between loving and liking. When Jesus said we are to love our enemies, He was speaking of an attitude higher than liking, because who can really like an enemy? We can love our enemies but not neccesarily like them.

Liking a person depends on many different aspects: on temperament, personality, and common interests. All of these factors have a bearing on whether we initially like someone. There are emotions that are involved in liking. Liking could be defined as 'the drawing together of people in an agreeable, enjoyable fellowship'. This is easy when we are dealing with co-operative family members or loyal friends, but not so easy when we are faced with those who have hurt or wronged us.

We need to be as practical as possible and not be satisfied with mere spiritual words. There is a quality of love that is beyond natural or family love. The Bible speaks

of agape love which is the divine love of God Himself
and which the Bible declares comes from the Holy Spirit:

*'And hope does not disappoint us, because God has
poured out his love into our hearts by the Holy Spirit,
whom he has given us.'*
(Romans 5:5)

Natural love comes from emotion. There are people
we love because of who they are. They are those with
whom we harmonize and feel a kindred spirit that is joyous and pleasant, but agape love comes from the will,
not merely from emotion. Agape love means 'a determi-
nation of the mind where we achieve an attitude of
unconquerable goodwill towards the one who may even
have seriously wronged us'. Another way of defining
agape love is 'the power to love those we do not like and
who do not like us'.

There is a difference between loving and liking.

It is painful and surprising for a preacher to discover
that there are people who do not like his ministry! I
heard an international preacher say on one occasion,
'I've had to learn that there are people who cannot
abide my ministry!' Most of us who preach and teach
like to think that everyone will enjoy and appreciate
what we say, but that is not so. We must, however, keep
an attitude of unconquerable goodwill towards those
who do not like us and who in turn we may not natur-
ally like. This is not being hypocritical. It is a genuine
operation of a principle of God.

If we treat a person as if we do like him, then this

releases agape love. It takes an operation of both the will and of the mind if we are to treat a person whom we do not like as if we really cared for him. We might say, 'How can we do that?' Well, we can, and I would like to illustrate how it is possible, from a very vivid personal experience.

As a young self-employed businessman, I had moved my office from one location to the fifth floor of a rather old building in the city where I then lived. It was a building that had an old-fashioned manually-operated lift. It was fitted with an interior metal folding gate and required the services of an operator in the busy working hours. The building was owned by a transport company. They had transferred one of the most aggressive and ill-mannered drivers in their employment to be the lift operator. This was because of his age and inability to handle heavy loads.

It was a semi-retirement job for this man, and the tenants in the building were totally dependent on him for the use of the elevator. He arrived early in the morning and left after office hours. I moved into the building happily thinking that I had a pleasant new office with a view from the fifth floor, but suddenly I met the impact of this man!

It would be impossible to really convey what he was like! He never smiled. He half lounged against the wall of the lift and when he did speak, his face would scowl, and he would grunt out some terse comment. I would greet him in the morning and say, 'Good morning.' There was only a grunt for a reply. 'It's a pleasant day.' Another grunt! When one pressed the call button, a bell rang in the lift, and if the operator was on another floor, he would take his time about coming. In fact, he would often walk along the passage before answering the call just to be difficult and unpleasant. By the time the elevator arrived at the appropriate floor, the intending passenger would often be furious! If a complaint was made, his unpleasantness increased. There was nothing one could do, because somehow the company who owned the building was willing to keep him employed in spite of his rudeness and lack of efficiency.

Day after day I would go to the elevator, ring the bell, wait, wait, and wait and finally the elevator would arrive. The door would be flung open. 'How are you?' I would say, and a grunt would be the only reply.

I had recently had a new experience of the Holy Spirit in my life and I had a deep desire to serve the Lord with all my heart. The operator could, however, make life difficult, so I suppose there was some self-preservation in my attitude, because if one got on the wrong side of this man he would take even longer than normal to come. I determined to keep up a barrage of goodwill toward him, and it must have been by the grace of God as I didn't understand the principles that I am now sharing.

I learnt to give him a warm greeting in spite of his rudeness. He would open the lift door and his unhappy face would look out. 'Good morning,' I would say, 'How are you?' The familiar grunt was the only reply. 'It's a pleasant day, did you have a good weekend?' Another grunt. I was determined to win! It became a game and a challenge day after day to say something cheerful and to greet him with goodwill.

Month after month I kept at it, and finally he began to respond with a smile and pleasant word and I began to see him as a hurt, wounded, and crippled man on the inside, not someone who was out to do everyone a bad turn.

This man did not know what it meant to like people, but when I came to move out of that building some years later, I had a relationship with him that was warm and pleasant, and I had even grown to like him. He was just as unpleasant with some other people, but I had won his respect by unconquerable goodwill. Some days the challenge was too much to face, and in the energy of my younger years, I bounded up the five flights of stairs rather than be confronted by that unpleasant man. It was not always easy to be cheerful to him, but I finally won. We can act toward a person as if we do like him and this releases divine love.

Another definition of agape love is 'the power to love those we do not like and who do not like us'.

When you have been hurt and need to forgive someone, let me challenge you; meditate on these six principles of how to forgive. If you fail and retain unforgiveness, you will be the one who will suffer. We know that it is vital to meditate on the Word of God, and it is important to meditate on these principles which are in harmony with what the Bible says.

Direct goodwill toward the person who has offended you, and keep on doing it! Don't say, 'Well, I tried to treat him kindly once and all I got back was an icy stare. That's it! I've done my part. It's over to him now!' No! The ball is always in our court. Keep on exercising goodwill and forgiving those who have offended you if you

want the continued blessing of the Lord in your own life.
Jesus said:

> *'But I tell you: Love your enemies and pray for those*
> *who who persecute you, that you may be sons of your*
> *Father in heaven...'*   (Matthew 5:44–45)

If we are blessing and praying for people, then something good is going to happen within us and also within them. Agape love does not just happen. We have to act in a positive way for divine love to flow through us.

When we obey the truths that have been set out, we will find it not only easy to forgive, but also to put out of our mind those thoughts that for years have negatively captured us. There is great power for good to be set in motion in our lives through genuine forgiveness. There is great power for harm if we do not forgive! The Living Bible gives this excellent paraphrase from Paul's letter to the Colossian church:

> *'Be gentle and ready to forgive; never hold grudges.*
> *Remember, the Lord forgave you, so you must forgive*
> *others.*
> *Most of all, let love guide your life, for then the whole*
> *church will stay together in perfect harmony.*
> *Let the peace of heart which comes from Christ be*
> *always present in your hearts and lives, for this is*
> *your responsibility and privilege as members of His*
> *body, and always be thankful.*
> *Remember what Christ taught and let His words*
> *enrich your lives and make you wise; teach them to*
> *each other and sing them out in psalms and hymns*
> *and spiritual songs, singing to the Lord with thankful*
> *hearts.'*   (Colossians 3:13–16)

We will find a new dimension of freedom when we learn to forgive. We will set in motion a flow of peace, health, joy, prosperity, and blessing. God wants us to enjoy His favour and His presence. He wants us to have the assurance that even in hard times He is training us to be mature sons and daughters. The scriptures are clear concerning our need to be forgiven by God, and our reponsibility to forgive others even if we are the offended party.

We cannot escape this responsibility if we want God's peace in our hearts. When we hold unforgiveness toward others it will inevitably bring problems into our lives. When we forgive others it will bring release to us. While we hold unforgiveness we become the prisoner of the person whom we will not forgive. Ill-will and bitterness can rise in our minds and the thought of that person and the wrong they may have done to us can be like a cancer that spreads its destructive tentacles into our entire being. God has been merciful to us, He has forgiven us, and pardoned us. Let us, in turn, be merciful and forgiving in all of our dealings with others.

There is great power for good to be set in motion in our lives through genuine forgiveness. There is great power for harm if we do not forgive!

Unforgiveness brings problems.
Forgiveness brings blessing.

If you have enjoyed this book please will you enable us to send a copy of it and many other titles, to a needy pastor in the **Third World**.

Please send your gift to:

> **Sovereign World Trust**
> **PO Box 777**
> **TONBRIDGE**
> **Kent TN4 0JF**
> **UK**

or to the **'Sovereign World'** distributor in your country. Please send International Money Order or Foreign Draft to **Sovereign World Trust**, in pounds, drawn on a UK bank.